FORENSICS *by the* *Stars*

ASTROLOGY INVESTIGATES

B.D. Salerno

iUniverse, Inc.
Bloomington

Forensics by the Stars
Astrology Investigates

iUniverse books may be ordered through booksellers or by contacting:

iUniverse
1663 Liberty Drive
Bloomington, IN 47403
www.iuniverse.com
1-800-Authors (1-800-288-4677)

ISBN: 978-1-4759-5602-3 (sc)
ISBN: 978-1-4759-5603-0 (hc)
ISBN: 978-1-4759-5604-7 (e)

Library of Congress Control Number: 2012919247

Printed in the United States of America

iUniverse rev. date: 10/22/2012

Contents

Acknowledgment

My heartfelt thanks go out to my dear friend-sister, Angela Dumas, and my sister-friend Cheryl Salerno, who believed that I could write this book even before I did, and for their unwavering support and encouragement during the insecure process of writing my first book.

I wish to thank my mother, Helen Salerno, for encouraging me at an early age to be a writer.

I also wish to thank my father, Loreto Salerno, a World War II veteran and former Air Force flight officer, who taught me how to navigate by the night sky. From him I learned my most valuable life lesson: when lost, seek direction from the stars.

Foreword

Forensic astrology is the interpretation of the energetic patterns of the zodiac signs, houses, stars, planets and other astrological configurations in a Horoscope to find clues to understanding personal and world events. I use forensic astrology to find out what happened in disturbing or mysterious circumstances like crimes, murders, missing persons and disasters. Event horoscopes can provide vital clues in an investigation. Here I have presented a selection of cases which illustrate the accuracy of astrological information about various crimes and cases which I have studied.

Many of my cases were taken from the news and some were from personal experience. With the exception of extremely well-known cases like the Lindbergh kidnapping and the death of Marilyn Monroe, I have changed the names of the victims to respect the privacy of the families.

This book is for fellow astrologers who wish to delve deeper into forensic astrology, newcomers to astrology and amateur detectives who wish to learn more about this divine science. For beginners I have included an Appendix of terms that I use frequently throughout the book whose concepts are important to understand. I also highly recommend the references listed in the Bibliography.

I also hope that investigators and detectives seeking alternate techniques for their work may take up the study of forensic astrology. Like threads of carpeting, blood spatter or fingerprints, forensic astrology can reveal an astonishing amount of detail about an event. This book only begins to scratch the surface. But let's begin.

Introduction

My fascination with astrology came at an early age. As a child, I was attracted to the night sky and its brilliant parade of the planets, the Moon and the stars. My most favorite of heavenly bodies was the brightest planet, Venus. I had no idea then that she was my ruling planet, or even that I was a Libran by birth. I just felt somehow connected to these distant bodies and stargazing became a favorite hobby.

My interest in astronomy did not go unnoticed by my family. On one crisp October birthday I received the most prized possession of my childhood – a telescope. It brought me even closer to my celestial companions and gave me many evenings of stargazing bliss.

But it wasn't just a fascination with the stars and planets that drew me to study this arcane science. It was the love of stories and the power the stars had to tell them. And no one in those early days told them better than my father. He had been a navigator in the Twentieth Air Force during World War II and had learned to navigate by the night skies, as many of his secret flight missions over the Pacific were conducted after dark.

So, when the evening stars rose, out we would go, and he would teach me the night sky.

I learned that by locating the upside-down chair of Cassiopeia, I could find Polaris, the North Star, how the three stars in the silvery belt of Orion the Hunter pointed southward to Sirius, the star of brightest magnitude, or northward to the Pleiades cluster. The stars were not random shimmering bodies against the backdrop of the indigo sky; they all fit together somehow, forming a cohesive pattern.

They, too, shared a story. And it didn't stop there. I began to discover that the stars and planets shared a rich legacy of mythological personalities – that they had an energy and virtual symbolic life all their own. The story of Cassiopeia is not just about a chair, but a spoiled princess whose chair was turned upside-down as a punishment for her vanity. Orion was a giant hunter so revered by Zeus that a constellation was created for him. Mars was not just a red planet, but the god of war and aggression; my favorite, Venus, was a goddess who celebrated harmony and beauty. The bright fixed star Spica indicated brilliance and success. Other fixed stars, like Bellatrix, in the Hunter's shoulder, foreshadowed war and danger. The night sky was an eternal stage and I was mesmerized by the roles its characters played.

I had already studied astrology for some time before I realized just how omniscient the heavens could be about matters here on earth. I took up the study of horary astrology in the early 1990s and was fascinated by the fact that astrology could actually answer questions that we don't know the answer to. It was then that I came across Barbara Watters' book *The Astrologer Looks At Murder,* which proposes the use of event charts to look further into the circumstances surrounding crimes. By just studying the charts of London's infamous Ripper murders in the 1880s, Ms. Watters developed a profile for Jack the Ripper and actually named the person whom she felt was responsible for the crimes, all based on astrology!

As an avid reader of true crime stories I was intrigued. It was also during this time that I began reading about the "Crime of the Century" – the kidnapping of the Lindbergh baby. And that was my first formal venture into the darkly fascinating world of forensic astrology.

CHAPTER ONE:

The Lindbergh Kidnapping

On March 1, 1932, Charles A. Lindbergh, Jr., baby son of the world famous aviator, was kidnapped from his East Amwell, New Jersey home, not far from my home town. Several weeks later the body of a baby was found in a wooded area about two miles from the home, which the coroner identified as Charles A. Lindbergh, Jr. A media firestorm ensued, culminating in the sensational trial and conviction of Bruno Hauptmann, a German immigrant carpenter from the Bronx, who steadfastly proclaimed his innocence until his last moments in the electric chair.

At that time, Lindbergh Sr. was enjoying superstar status in the media, having won acclaim by being the first aviator to complete a non-stop transcontinental flight in 1927 in his aircraft The Spirit of St. Louis. The kidnapping of the child was met with horror and anger by an adoring public. The trial was a media feeding frenzy attended by journalists from around the world. Such was its historic impact that re-enactments still take place at the Hunterdon County Courthouse in Flemington, New Jersey.

I was fascinated by the story of this crime and wanted to try my hand at reading my first forensic horoscope. The resulting chart was revealing, if not startling, in its descriptiveness. See the "Lindbergh Kidnapping" horoscope on page 8.

In my studies of horary and event astrology I relied heavily on the writings of seventeenth century astrologer, William Lilly, and earlier classical astrologers. As Lilly suggested below, I cast my chart for the time the child was discovered missing and followed his advice from his *Introduction to Astrology*:

"Of a thing suddenly happening, whether it signifies Good or Evil?

"Erect your figure of heaven at the exact time of any event happening, or when you first heard of it: then consider who is Lord of the ascendant, and which planet disposes of Sun and Moon; and see if either of these be in the ascendant; and if more than one, take the most powerful; and let his position be well considered. If he be in good aspect with Sun, Jupiter or Venus; there will no evil arise from the accident, rumour, or whatever the event may be; but if you find that planet weak in the scheme, combust, or in evil aspect to Uranus, Saturn, Mars or Mercury, there will some evil occur."[1]

The chart was cast for 9:50 PM on March 1, 1932 in East Amwell, N.J. In the crime chart the horoscope Ascendant, or rising sign, is Libra. In an event or crime chart, the person in question or the missing person is shown as the Ascendant and the planet ruling that sign. Venus rules Libra, so besides the Ascendant itself, we must look to the position and quality of Venus to find more information about the person. Venus will be in a sign and house which will further describe the person and his condition. If Venus is well-placed, we may have nothing further to worry about. But not in the case of little Charlie. We know from history that Charlie died sometime during or after the kidnapping, but from an astrological perspective the horoscope confirms this, and in chilling detail.

We look to Venus, its sign and house placement, its dignities, including triplicity, term and face, and aspects it makes to the other planets, and whether or not it is conjoined to one of the fixed stars. Armed with this checklist, and Lilly's rules, I studied Venus to see what it had to reveal about the fate of little Charlie. As my first venture into this method, it didn't take long for me to be astonished at the findings. Everything spells extreme danger, and death, for the child:

- Venus is in the late degrees of the sign Aries, indicating a critical condition
- Venus is in Aries, sign of its detriment, signifying ineffectiveness and weakness and showing that Charlie had little power over his fate
- Venus is disposited by Mars, a traditional malefic which represents violence, disruptiveness, brutality, strife
- Venus is in terms of this violent Mars
- Venus is in the sixth house of accidents, servitude, illness
- Venus also rules the eighth house of death, because of its rulership of Taurus
- Venus is in a stressful square aspect to Pluto, planet of destruction
- Venus separates from conjunction with Uranus, planet of accidents
- Venus is conjunct the malefic fixed star Baten Kaitos

In his book *Star Names and Their Meanings*, Richard Hinckley Allen says of this fixed star "... in astrology, it portends falls and blows."[2] As I would learn over and over again the fixed star testimonies can be quite literal.

Little Charlie's remains were found on May 12, several weeks after his disappearance, in a field about two miles from the East Amwell home. The child's skull bore evidence of a large fracture, the result of accidental or deliberate blunt force trauma.

Charlie had been taken from the nursery on the second floor of his home. According to the police report the kidnapper had performed the acrobatic feat of scaling a ladder to the window of the nursery, opening the window, entering the room, snatching the child from his crib—where he was covered by a blanket secured to the bedding by safety pins—removing the child noiselessly, exiting the window with the baby in tow, and descending the ladder to the ground. The ladder was found alongside the house with a lower rung broken in half. Many speculated that when descending the ladder with the child in tow, the rung broke, sending both kidnapper and child to the ground in a disastrous fall. In any case, the child suffered a crushing blow to the head, which proved fatal.

In this first forensic analysis, there is already have enough information to confirm that the child is deceased, having suffered a fatal blow to the head. Venus, the child's planet, is in the sign Aries, which rules the head, and separates from conjunction with Uranus, planet of accidents, and squares Pluto, planet of destruction. Aries is ruled by Mars, which is the perpetrator's sign. The child was completely controlled by his abductor, as we would expect. But by just analyzing the placement and dignities of Venus I had already figured out a great deal about this unfortunate incident.

I was hooked—there was definitely something to this method of working with horoscopes. Since I was able to glean so much information about the child, I then turned to the Descendant to see what I could find out about the perpetrator.

The facts of the crime clearly suggested that more than one person was involved, and evidence of collaboration among the members of the Lindbergh household was apparent. The kidnapping occurred on a Tuesday night, which the family normally spent at their main home in Englewood, N.J. However, little Charlie had been suffering from a cold, so it was decided not to make to trip to the north Jersey suburb, where he normally would have been that night. How did the kidnapper know that the child would be in East Amwell and not Englewood? Only someone within the household would have been privy to the sudden change in plans.

Violet Sharp, a housemaid at the Englewood residence, behaved very strangely when first questioned by police. When they returned for a second questioning, she panicked and committed suicide by drinking a bottle of silver polish on the spot. This left many to speculate that she had been involved in the plot, even if to just tip off the kidnapper that Charlie was in East Amwell that night, and not Englewood.

The crime chart suggests collusion. The perpetrator is shown by 29 degrees Aries on the seventh house; its ruler is Mars, which is in Pisces in the fifth house of children. The presence of other planets conjoining Mars in the fifth house describes a gang or group of conspirators. Mars in Pisces is in opposition to shady Neptune. An aspect between these two planets is descriptive of a kidnapping or abduction. In addition, Mars rules the sixth house of servants as well as the seventh of the abductor. The nature of the crime required cooperation from someone within the home and the participation by a servant is reinforced in the event chart.

It would have been very difficult for one person to scale the ladder up to the second floor of the Lindbergh home, open the window, step off into the baby's room, remove the baby from his crib, exit through the window with baby in tow, maneuver his way back onto the top rung of the ladder, gain a solid footing and then descend the ladder clutching the child in one arm and the ladder in the other. It would have been easier, faster, and quieter for one of the servants to simply open the window and hand the child to the kidnapper on the ladder. Or for the kidnapper to have entered the residence on foot, avoiding a perilous climb up an obviously shaky ladder. This too would have required cooperation from inside the home. As it turned out, the descent down the shaky ladder was dangerous enough that a rung broke, sending kidnapper and baby into a disastrous fall. This may be what caused the child's fractured skull. With the sixth house emphasis and with Venus separating from conjunction with Uranus an accident is a very strong possibility.

While Violet Sharp's behavior stirred immediate suspicion, there was the possibility of another servant being involved, one in the East Amwell household who participated directly in the affair. The grouping of planets in Pisces reinforces this idea: ruler of sixth house, servants, in the fifth house of children, places the responsibility for the child in the hands of the servants. A kidnapping of this nature and its timing would require some collusion from within the household, and the horoscope supports the idea that a few people were involved.

I didn't know it then, but came to find in many subsequent crime horoscopes, that a Mars-Neptune opposition usually signifies kidnapping. Obviously, in the Lindbergh case we already know this. But in a cold case or case of a missing person who has not been found, this can be invaluable information, as not all who go missing are the victims of kidnapping or even foul play. For example, in a cold case of a disappearance where there is no information available, the Mars-Neptune opposition may point toward kidnapping or abduction, rather than a person simply going off of their own free will. Astrology can provide valuable clues to investigations of this nature.

I was also astounded when I examined the chart for information about Charles Sr. The father is shown by the fourth house, with Aquarius on its cusp. Charles Sr. is represented by Saturn, at zero degrees Aquarius, which is conjunct the fixed star Altair, in the constellation Aquila, the "Flying Eagle." Eerily, Charles Lindbergh's flying prowess had earned him his nickname "the Flying Eagle." The fact that the event horoscope described Lindbergh's nickname gave me the chills. This was the first of many times where specific details of an event resonated with fixed stars prominent in the chart. Baten Kaitos and Altair give precise information about the nature of the child's injury and his father, both of which are confirmed by evidence in the case.

Charles Sr.'s Saturn is a powerful planet in this chart. It is at a critical zero degree, in its own triplicity, term and sign of its rulership. It is also angular, being within five degrees of the fourth house cusp. Charles Sr. controlled the outcome of this case from the start. The newly formed New Jersey State Police allowed him full authority over the investigation, an unprecedented and questionable move. He directed the course of the investigation and his instructions were followed by police and investigators far more experienced than he was in such matters. This was a testament to the enormous charisma and respect that he commanded over an adoring and worshipping public, but it remains one of the more peculiar, and curious, aspects of the case.

I did much more investigating into the Lindbergh horoscope, but that has become the basis for another writing project which will explore the case in more detail. The present analysis offers a glimpse into my first experience with forensic astrology and the immediate impact it had on my present work.

This new knowledge of forensic astrology excited me and stirred my interest to learn more. If the stars could teach me so much about a case in which the celestial clues were confirmed by fact, what could I discover about cases where the facts of the crime were uncertain or unknown?

There was one disturbing and untimely death that had had a tremendous impact on me as a child. It remained a source of speculation for many years to come, and was never resolved to the satisfaction of thousands of grieving fans, including myself. I had long pondered, was it really suicide? Was it an accident? Or was it murder? Armed with my new knowledge of forensics by the stars, I relied on their investigative powers once again to find out what really happened to Marilyn Monroe.

Lindbergh Kidnapping

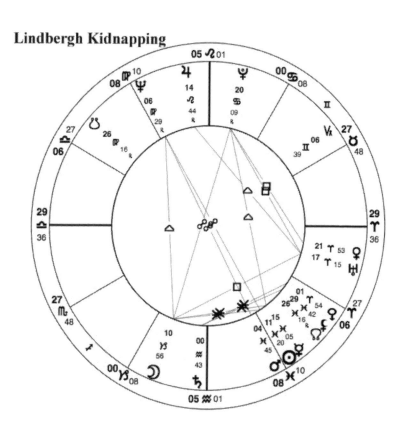

Endnotes

1 Lilly, William. *Introduction to Astrology,* Original publication 1647, Delhi: A. Sagar, Book House, 1993, 96.

2 Allen, Richard Hinckley. *Star Names and Their Meanings,* New York: G.E. Stechert, 1899, 163.

Chapter Two

The Murder of Marilyn Monroe

F ew women in the history of the world evoke an image as
enduring as that of Marilyn Monroe. She remains one of the
most captivating cultural icons of the Twentieth Century, certainly
best known for her sensually provocative, yet emotionally fragile
persona. Her death, fifty years ago, continues to captivate us and
haunt us.

The official account is that she committed suicide by
ingesting a lethal dose of sleeping pills. The autopsy report read,
"acute barbiturate poisoning," "ingestion of overdose," and the
indeterminate "probable suicide."[1] But still, conspiracies abound:
Some claim she was murdered by the Kennedys, the CIA, or the
Mafia. Others believe that she succumbed to an accidental overdose,
or that her death was the result of medical malpractice. Can
astrology help clarify the suspicious circumstances surrounding
this mystery?

I grew up during the sixties and still recall feeling the shock
of the announcement of her death over the radio. Years later,
as I gained experience as a forensic astrologer, I began to study
the charts of mysterious and unexplained events, and Marilyn's
suspicious death topped the list. After extensive research, and
after studying the event chart of her last evening, I joined the

legions of fans and admirers who believe that Marilyn Monroe was not the victim of suicide, but of murder.

Marilyn departed this life on the evening of August 4, 1962, having turned thirty-six years of age just two months earlier. We know from accounts of that evening that Marilyn passed away some time around 10:30 PM.[2] Why then, with her housekeeper in attendance along with two doctors, were the police not telephoned until 4:35 the following morning? Why were Marilyn's psychiatrist, Dr. Ralph Greenson, and internist Dr. Hyman Engelberg, called to Marilyn's home hours before the police? It was in fact Dr. Engelberg who placed the call at 4:35 AM to notify the police of Marilyn's death.[3] See the event horoscope at the end of the chapter.

The housekeeper, Mrs. Eunice Murray, was the main witness to the events of this disturbing evening, but proved to be the most unreliable. She claimed that she found Marilyn dead in her bed around midnight, but later said that the bedroom door was locked, so that the doctors had to break the window from outside to gain entry. She also saw a light on under the bedroom door, which alarmed her. However, further inspection of the bedroom showed that Mrs. Murray could not have seen a light shining from under Marilyn's door as she had claimed.[4] It's a very suspicious scenario, and we haven't even gotten to the event chart yet!

The event chart shows 21 degrees Cancer rising. In her birth chart Cancer is on the cusp of Marilyn's natal twelfth house, so that at this time her twelfth house is rising. The twelfth house in astrology describes secrecy, cover-ups, self-undoing and hidden enemies, an apt description for the events of this evening.

Cancer's ruler, the Moon, also represents Marilyn and controls the fourth house of endings. Its ruler Venus is very weak: she is cadent, in late degrees of Virgo, in her fall, void of course, in terms of Saturn (the natural ruler of death), and in trine to Saturn which here also rules the eighth house of death. Together, these all spell out a grim message: Marilyn is gone, and nothing can be done to save her. But the other planets also have their story to tell.

In an event chart the seventh house reveals information about open enemies, and we look to it for clues about the perpetrator(s).

The cusp of the seventh is 21 degrees Capricorn. It is in close proximity to the Arabic Lot, or Part, of Poisoned Things: a fatal dose of drugs, or poison, was administered by someone other than Marilyn. The official cause of death was acute barbiturate poisoning, with excessive amounts of pentobarbital (as found in the sleep drug Nembutal) and chloral hydrate. So toxic was the dosage administered that Marilyn could not have lived long enough to ingest all of it orally.[5] The drugs therefore had to have been administered by enema or injection – which challenges the case for suicide and sets the stage for murder.

Saturn rules the seventh house and is the strongest planet in the chart, suggesting a powerful person who had a firm control over Marilyn, especially during the last hours of her life. Interesting that in classical astrology Saturn rules death, whether natural or otherwise, and here also rules the eighth house of death.

Saturn is in the terms of Mercury, which rules psychiatric doctors. It is conjunct the Dragon's Tail or South Node of the Moon, another unfortunate placement in astrology. The planets are telling us that in this event, Marilyn's last hours were controlled by someone powerful who directly caused her death by acute drug poisoning. Who else could prescribe and administer these drugs but her doctor?

What is Marilyn's relationship with him? Her planet, the Moon, forms a close 120-degree angle, or trine, with Saturn. She knew her murderer, in fact, she revered him greatly: Moon in Libra was in the sign of exaltation of Saturn—perhaps she revered him a little more than he deserved, as an exaltation will often show. Marilyn was very close to her doctor and had become increasingly dependent on him to provide her with narcotics that would help her sleep. But the doctor was not the only one in attendance that night. Mrs. Murray admitted years later that Robert Kennedy had paid a visit to Marilyn, and he was also seen entering and leaving her home by neighbors on that evening.[6] Does the horoscope make reference to Kennedy's role in her death?

Saturn, the power planet of the chart, ruler of the perpetrator, is in square aspect to Neptune, suggesting confusion, deception and cover-up. Indeed no one to this day really has the real inside story of exactly what happened, and that in itself is true to Neptune's elusive nature. The murderer engaged in trickery to stage a suicide scene, when in fact the fatal poisons could only have been given by someone other than Marilyn. But why?

It is well noted in several biographies of Marilyn that she had had affairs with both Kennedy brothers and that she was now a liability in terms of what she knew about secret affairs at the White House. According to reports, she had kept a diary containing sensitive information about world affairs that she had discussed with them and had threatened to make the information public. This is the basis for the theory that she was murdered and that the murder was staged as a suicide. Does the event chart give any traction to this theory?

The autopsy report stated that Marilyn had died while lying face down on the bed with the telephone receiver grasped in one hand. Lividity, which occurs when blood begins to pool in a part of the body after death, was present on the front of the body. But there was also evidence of bruising on both arms and on her right hip.[7] Was this the result of being shaken by her doctor in an attempt to wake her from a drug-induced state? Or was she held down and injected with enough narcotics to kill several people? Deception among the witnesses is also borne out by the chart. The sixth house rules servants and housekeepers. Marilyn's housekeeper, Mrs. Murray, is shown by the sixth house and its ruler Jupiter, which is in the sign of Pisces, a sign often associated with sacrifice and denial. When afflicted, it brings confusion, deception and vagueness. Here Jupiter is opposed by Pluto: the housekeeper may have been manipulated or coerced into making false statements. Jupiter also trines elusive Neptune, facilitating secrecy and a cover-up. I believe Mrs. Murray was forced to hide the real truth of what happened that night. With her planet Jupiter in its own terms, her main interest was self-preservation at the expense of obscuring the truth. Years later, she continued to contradict her accounts of what happened that night.

Mrs. Murray's inconsistent testimony is paralleled by that of law enforcement officials who investigated the case. They too are ruled by ninth-house Jupiter and their role in the deception can't be ruled out. The telephone records of that night, which would have established a critical timeline for calls that Marilyn received and made, were lost or destroyed. In addition, some of Marilyn's organ samples went missing after the autopsy[8] and these are all crucial evidence in determining more precise information about her death.

There is a very strong reference to brothers in the chart, as evidenced by the placement of planets which refer to JFK and RFK. In the event chart Mars rules the fifth house of love affairs and the tenth house of the President, a world leader. The President's brother is shown by the twelfth house. The twelfth house is ruled by Mercury, which is also the natural ruler of brothers. Mercury disposits Mars, showing one brother's influence over the other. The position of Mars on the twelfth indicates someone in hiding or someone whose presence was kept secret. We will see this position elsewhere in crime charts. In this chart, I believe it suggests the presence of Bobby Kennedy during this evening of suspicious, secretive events.

But the most revealing aspect of the chart is not just in the disposition of the planets. The Ascendant, at 21 degrees Cancer, is straddled on both sides by the twin fixed stars Castor and Pollux. The narrative of astrology is quite literal, and this position of the fixed stars speaks volumes about Marilyn's situation at the time of her death.

In Greek mythology Castor and Pollux were siblings, Castor representing the feminine, spiritual sister, and Pollux being the more violent brother. Pollux was a boxer, an enforcer of sorts. German astrologer Ebertin-Hoffman called him "the wicked boy."[9]

Marilyn had been involved in love affairs with both the Kennedy brothers, most recently prior to her death, Bobby

Kennedy. Neptune is conjunct the fifth house cusp; the affairs were conducted in strict secrecy and their revelation could have brought down Camelot. Like the Ascendant framed by the pair of fixed stars, Marilyn was caught between two powerful men who had everything to lose if their indiscretions were made public.

Mars in this secretive position also gives rise to more speculation: could it suggest an injection (puncture) into an arm, or worse, into a lung (Gemini)? No such puncture wounds were found at autopsy, but neither were some of Marilyn's organs after they were removed from her body, so how can we really trust the official accounts of what took place? We can only surmise from the event horoscope that in death, as in life, Marilyn was caught between powerful brothers who felt they could not afford for their indiscretions to be exposed and a doctor who had at his disposal enough drugs to kill her many times over.

Even today, the fiftieth anniversary of Marilyn's death, many still mourn her and want to know what really happened. Her fame now far eclipses her popularity at the time of her death, and last year her estate was rated the third most prosperous in Forbes' annual list of top deceased celebrities.[10] Marilyn's journey was brief and ultimately tragic, but she summed it up best herself. In a sarcastic note sent on June 13, 1962, to Robert and Ethel Kennedy after her firing by Twentieth Century-Fox just weeks before her death, she quipped:

".... Unfortunately I am involved in a freedom ride protesting the loss of the minority rights belonging to the few remaining earthbound stars. After all, all we demanded was our right to twinkle."[11] She won back those rights from Fox, only to succumb just weeks later to overpowering forces, both planetary and human. But as it has already done, her right to twinkle, and her star power, will surpass many lifetimes.

Marilyn Monroe

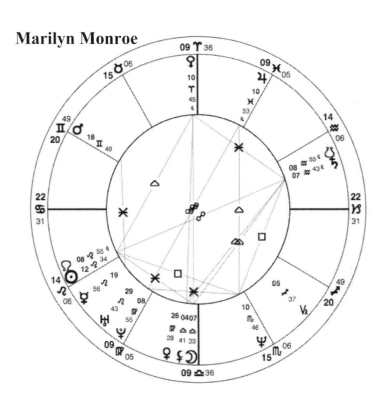

ENDNOTES

1 Speriglio, Milo. *Marilyn Monroe Murder Cover-Up*, (Van Nuys: Seville Publishing, 1982), 260.

2 Wolfe, Donald E. *The Last Days of Marilyn Monroe*, (New York: William Morrow and Company, Inc., 1998), 29.

3 Speriglio, *op. cit.*, 56.

4 *Ibid*, 44.

5 Wolfe, *op. cit.*, 42.

6 Margolis, Jay. *Marilyn Monroe: A Case for Murder*, (Bloomington: iUniverse, Inc., 2011), 232.

7 Speriglio, *op. cit.*, 56.

8 Wolfe, *op. cit.*, 34.

9 Ebertin-Hoffman, Reinhold. *Fixed Stars and Their Interpretations*, (Tempe: American Federation of Astrologers, 1971), 41.

10 Anthony McCartney, *Marilyn Monroe - Still a Celebrity Brand 50 Years Later*, http://www.huffingtonpost.com (August 3, 2012).

11 Margolis, *op. cit.*, 68.

CHAPTER THREE:

Missing Persons, Mysterious Deaths

This chapter is about the unfortunate events that make up the majority of the cases which I study. Often when I hear of a tragic death in the news, an unexplained murder or a missing person, I draw up a horoscope to learn more about what happened. The following sections were taken from my files and illustrate how forensic astrology can provide clues to current and cold cases.

I have also included a few cases of accidental death and suicide to illustrate the patterns that are present in the forensic horoscopes of such misfortunes.

Imagine if police or investigative departments could avail themselves of these powerful techniques! If police are sometimes willing to employ psychics, they should also be aware of the possibilities of working with astrologers. I believe that astrology and law enforcement could make a formidable combination in discovering revealing information about crimes and cold cases.

The cases in this chapter were taken from my files to illustrate various techniques in determining whether a missing person is dead or alive, whether they may return safely; if murdered, the likely cause of death, and profiles of the perpetrator. I have changed the names of the victims and some details of these cases out of respect for the privacy of the victims' families and friends. Although I have worked with investigators in several missing persons and cold cases in the recent past, I have not included those cases here as some of them are ongoing and the information is confidential.

All of the cases discussed in this book are solely for the purpose of sharing valuable information on how to work with the astrology of such events. It is useful to keep Lilly's advice in mind, which was quoted in Chapter One. As a rule, I follow these steps when working with crime charts:

- determine the state and quality of the Ascendant and its ruler, which represents the victim,
- note afflictions to the Moon, which signify danger and matters going badly
- afflictions to Saturn show cruelty, injury and often death
- to Mars, violence and bloodshed,
- to Uranus, catastrophic accidents,
- to Neptune, confusion, deceit, overdose and/or addiction
- to Pluto, destruction and upheaval

If associated with the Ascendant, a well-placed Jupiter or Venus is a hopeful signs that the person is alive and safe. Look to the seventh house and its ruler for the description of the wrongdoer. Now let's put the rules together to study a few horoscopes of missing persons.

Jean

One September morning just after the fall semester began, a promising college senior, whom we'll call Jean, entered a campus dormitory and was never seen again. I cast an event horoscope for the time she was last seen entering her dorm.

She is shown by the 27 degree Libra Ascendant, and by Venus, Libra's ruler, in the tenth house. The placement of Venus shows she was quite proud of her academic accomplishments and enthusiastic about her future career. Venus in Leo describes a warm, caring person who is liked by many. However, 27 degrees on the Ascendant are critical, giving the chart an ominous introduction. What became of this promising young student after she entered her dorm that morning, and why was she not seen again? At first glance I was concerned that Jean would not be seen alive again. The Moon's South Node, known to the ancients as "Cauda Draconis" or "Dragon's Tail," is an indicator of difficulty or tragedy, and here it is conjunct the Midheaven of this chart. Her fate is a public tragedy. The South Node occupies 29 degrees of Cancer, another critical degree placement which warns of heartbreak in the family.

Venus, her ruler, also rules the eighth house of death. As in the case of baby Lindbergh discussed earlier, if the Ascendant ruler also rules the eighth house it is an ominous sign.

The next placement that struck me was Mercury, just inside the twelfth house, and retrograde in Libra. I felt there was someone lying in wait in her dorm. Because the planet is in Libra, ruled by Jean's planet Venus, I felt this person liked her a great deal, but she did not return the affection—Venus in Leo did not reciprocate Mercury's favor. Jean had been friendly with this person, but was not interested in him romantically; she already had a boyfriend whom she was planning to marry after graduation.

This Mercury-person also rules the eighth house Part of Fortune and the ninth house of higher education. He controlled the outcome of this disappearance in a bad way. I believe Jean was confronted by another student and assaulted for personal and emotional reasons. Mars, ruler of the seventh of the perpetrator, is in the ninth (again, another student or colleague) in Cancer. Mars is in its fall in Cancer. A planet in its fall is ignored, overlooked, ineffective, an apt description for the attacker, as we will see.

To add more darkness to this picture, Mars is separating from opposition with Pluto and is squared by the retrograde Mercury: a quick, violent assault befell her from an emotionally unstable friend whose feelings she did not reciprocate. This is reinforced by the Moon in Taurus in the seventh house of the perpetrator. With Venus exalted in Taurus, this person had a strong emotional investment in her, but she was involved with someone else, cause for an unstable person to feel abandoned and resentful.

Sadly, a few days after she went missing, Jean's lifeless body was found hidden away in the dorm lavatory. A fellow student eventually confessed to the crime, and revealed that he had harbored intense feelings for her which she had not reciprocated.

Because the malefic fixed star Caput Algol is on the eighth house cusp, I believed Jean had been strangled, and the opposition of Mars to Pluto is testimony that a sexual assault was attempted. These unfortunate facts were borne out by the autopsy. This was a very disturbing case to work on. The murderer was apprehended, so that Jean's tragic death will not go unpunished.

Jean

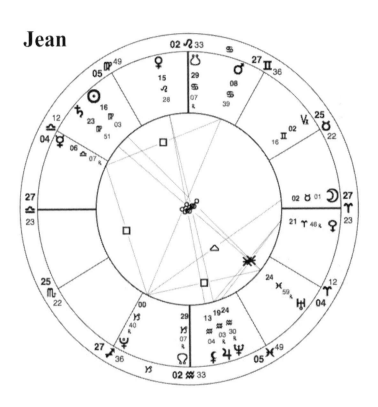

TIM

An eleven-year-old boy mysteriously disappeared from his home on an autumn morning a few years ago. I cast the chart for the last time that he was seen by a neighbor. We'll call him Tim.

When I work on horoscopes of child abductions, I usually hope for the best but expect the worst. This time I was very pleased to find that there were no aspects to indicate a tragic ending for Tim. Why? The rising sign is Scorpio, so the child is ruled by Mars in Cancer in the ninth house. Mars is very weak, in its fall in Cancer and in a cadent house. Tim suffered from asthma and other debilitating health problems that could become life-threatening if he were not found quickly. He cannot help himself. But Mars is also in the terms of Jupiter, a beneficial planet. This is an encouraging sign that nothing harmful has happened to him. Mars is not in hard aspect to Saturn, or the rulers of the sixth or twelfth houses. It is in square to Mercury, ruler of the eighth house, so there are some concerns about his safety. However while the boy's ruler is weak, neither it nor the Moon are afflicted by the malefics. He was not in control of his destiny, but I held out hope that he might be alive and safe.

In his condition he would not have been able to run away on his own, so I looked to the seventh house to find out more about his abductor. The ruler of the seventh house is Venus in Leo in the tenth. This shows that the abductor had some authority over the boy, or some kind of a parental type of caregiver relationship. Venus is in the terms of the Sun and Jupiter so I don't sense that this person had bad intentions. But Venus is also opposed by Jupiter and Neptune in the fourth house, so the perpetrator had the misguided intention of helping or saving him from something, as he was literally removed from his home (opposition from tenth to fourth house of the home). Misguided though it was, a Venus-Jupiter opposition is much less threatening than an opposition to Saturn, Uranus, or Pluto.

So where did Tim end up? Mars in the ninth says that he was far away before being discovered. In fact the day after his disappearance he was found a hundred miles away with an older friend from the same community. The two had shared a brotherly relationship and the adult had taken him from his home and brought him away unharmed. It was a misguided act, but not a malicious one. Tim was later returned home safely.

It was gratifying to work on a horoscope like this with a happy ending, where the missing child returns home safely. I wish all the horoscopes for missing children that I work on would turn out this way.

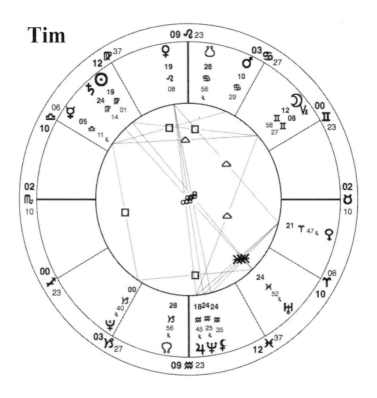

JOAN

In the spring of 2009 Joan, an attractive 19-year-old college sophomore, went for a weekend getaway with some friends and has not been seen since. I constructed the horoscope from the time she was last seen at a popular resort. The astrological findings suggest that a group of her peers may have been involved in her disappearance, and the focus of the horoscope is therefore on the connections between Joan's ruling planet and the seventh house of the perpetrator/abductor.

Joan is shown by the rising sign, Scorpio, and Scorpio's ruler, Mars, which is in Aries in the fifth house. This describes her as an active, outgoing teen who was having a good time on this vacation. Mars is in its own sign, Aries—she was into enjoying herself, and not another person. Unfortunately Aries is considered a "violent" sign in crime astrology so there is a shadow of concern for her safety.

Libra is the seventh house sign, and its ruler of the perp/abductor is Venus. In fact Mars, Joan's planet, and Venus, planet of the perpetrator are conjoined in the fifth house of recreation. The Mars/Venus placement in Aries is important: Venus, planet of the perp, in Joan's sign shows that the person involved in her disappearance was interested in her. A planet in another planet's sign shows interest, even attraction. But Joan's planet Mars is in its own sign: the feelings were not reciprocated. Joan's abductor may have expressed interest, and was likely refused. Venus in Aries wants what it wants and is not particularly patient in waiting to receive it. Here Venus is literally pursuing Mars in the fifth house of sex. Both meet up with a square to Pluto, indicating a possible sexual assault.

There are others involved as well, shown by Sun, Moon and Mercury in the seventh house of the abductor. Possibly three others were involved or had knowledge of the crime. These people are controlled by the main offender and are loyal to him: they are ruled by his planet Venus. Saturn, traditional ruler of death, is exactly conjunct the eleventh house cusp of friends and associates. Mercury, which rules the eighth house of death as well as the eleventh house of friends, is exactly conjunct the evil fixed star Caput Algol. The literal meaning of Algol is losing one's head, and can also indicate suffocation or strangulation. It is unfortunately often seen in charts involving heinous crimes and devastating events.

To date Joan has not been found but leads are being developed which point to one individual who had in fact been hanging out with others at the resort. There is in fact more than one person of interest, as the astrology of the event has told us.

Unfortunately, as of this writing, Joan has not been found, and there is insufficient evidence to indict any of her acquaintances. The astrology of the case suggests that the persons of interest were acquainted with her and others have knowledge of what happened. Hopefully one of them will come forward.

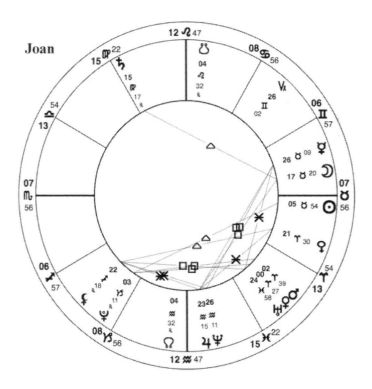

JILL

Most of the crime horoscopes that I work on describe tragic circumstances, but this particular case of a missing six-year-old had a happy ending. Jill was last seen playing in the front yard of her home with her brother. Suddenly a stranger pulled up to the yard, knocked the brother down, grabbed Jill and sped away in his car. I cast the chart for the time the police were called.

Jill is ruled by Jupiter which is in Aquarius in the third house and her valiant brother is ruled by Saturn, which rules the third house in this chart. The third house is the house of siblings. This placement shows that the brother was responsible for the six-year-old and struggled to protect her. Saturn at the Midheaven also lends an authoritarian role to him. The brother fought for Jill but the intruder won and drove away with Jill in tow.

It was encouraging that Jupiter was not afflicted by the usual signs of violence or death and I took this as a promising sign. It appeared that Jill might actually be unharmed. Since Mercury, the intruder's sign, was retrograde, I felt he would be caught soon and that perhaps the little girl would be found alive.

What else about the perp? Mercury in Gemini shows he is a young person. Venus and Mars straddling the fifth house of children, in my experience, often describes a sex offender. Mercury is exactly zero degrees Gemini, but retrograding into Taurus. Mercury is leaving its home sign and backing into a sign where it is peregrine or lost: the perp is just beginning to lose control to his perverted passion. But happily, both the perp and the girl were found the very next day in a town just ten miles east of her home. If there can be a "best expression" of a child offender it may have been that Mercury had been in its own dignity, and so the perp did not harm her. He turned out to be a 27-year-old registered sex offender and was arrested for her abduction. Thankfully little Jill was returned safely to her family and Jupiter's benevolent promise was fulfilled.

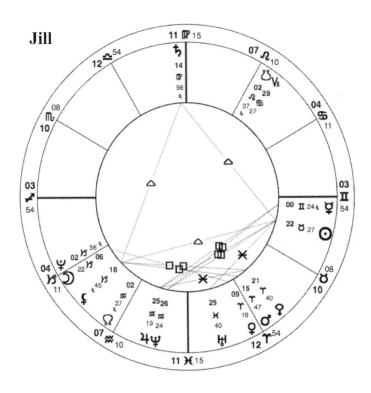

JANE

This young mother of three children went missing from her home just before the Christmas holidays. Her purse, cell phone and keys were still in her home. Her husband claimed that she up and left the family without warning. I used the time she was reportedly last seen to cast the horoscope.

The Ascendant provides some insights as to the young woman's whereabouts at this time. She is shown by Mercury in the fourth house, which has just entered the sign of Capricorn. She was in her home but the fact that Mercury had just changed signs from Sagittarius to Capricorn is significant. Mercury in in its detriment in Sagittarius, so she was troubled and felt like she could not control her situation. Mercury moved into Capricorn, where her troubles came to a head. Capricorn's ruler is Saturn in Libra in the first house, representing concerns over a relationship, possible marital troubles and feeling extremely burdened by them. Saturn is in square to Pluto which describes a destructive situation.

With Mercury's move into Capricorn she may have voiced her discontent, as Mercury squares Saturn, but it is also approaching the planet of destruction, Pluto, which also squares Saturn. The disagreement ended up being devastating. This is not the chart of someone who has taken a sudden trip on a lark without her purse, cell phone or keys. Something much more serious took place.

The seventh house in astrology rules the spouse, partnerships of all kinds and also your "open enemies," those who are known to you. Unfortunately the partner can also end up being an enemy in a difficult marriage. What does the seventh house reveal here?

Uranus, a volatile and often explosive planet, is on the seventh house cusp. Uranus rules sudden accidents, break-ups and divorce. Possibly a divorce was the subject of a heated discussion. It also describes the state of mind of the partner as being erratic and prone to sudden action.

The partner is shown by Jupiter in Aquarius in the fifth house. The partner is concerned over his children. Jupiter opposes Mars in Leo so the partner may have recently overreacted or lost his temper. Jupiter is conjunct Neptune, planet of confusion and deception. Jupiter also rules the fourth house, end of the matter.

The chart describes a violent incident, possibly blunt force trauma to the head (Aries on eighth house of death suggests a violent end and Saturn suggests a blow or crushing). This is not a promising chart for finding her alive, and she has not been found to this day.

In the weeks following her disappearance, many came to suspect her husband, who steadfastly denied his innocence. In my view, the horoscope does suggest the possibility of involvement by the husband. Unfortunately, we will never know. Some time after Jane's disappearance the husband committed suicide by blowing himself up in his car, sadly fulfilling the promise of the volatile, explosive Uranus that described him.

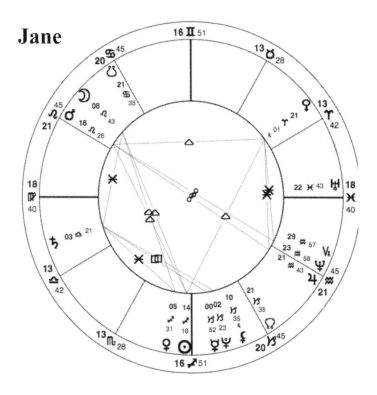

JIMMY

A four-year-old boy, Jimmy, was reported missing by his mother after both attended a friend's birthday party. I lived near the area at that time and remember how the story dominated the media. To this day, no one has been apprehended for the crime, much to the frustration of detectives who strongly suspected foul play on the mother's part. The astrology of the event points to a tragic death and a cover-up which may go unpunished.

The fixed stars send a grim message from this event horoscope. Antares is rising on the Ascendant of this chart, suggesting recklessness and danger. Jupiter, the Ascendant ruler, represents Jimmy. It is found in the eighth house of death, in opposition to Saturn, natural ruler of death. The child is also shown by Mars, ruler of the fifth house of children. Here Mars is in its fall, in the eighth house, at critical 29 degrees of Cancer. The horoscope strongly points to foul play resulting in Jimmy's death.

The horoscope paints another disturbing picture of the circumstances surrounding Jimmy's last hours: there is a Grand Cross in fixed signs, formed by Moon in Scorpio opposite Mercury in Taurus, crossed by Saturn in Aquarius opposite Jupiter in Leo. In astrology the Moon can represent the mother: her behavior was suspicious after the crime, and she changed her story many times when interviewed by police, who came to suspect her but were unable to come up with any solid evidence. The Moon in Scorpio reveals her as secretive and obstructive. Scorpio is one of the three "mute" signs in Astrology, the other being companion water signs Cancer and Pisces. The mother never spoke about what really happened, other than to blame the abduction on individuals whose existence was questionable. She also gave conflicting accounts of what happened when questioned by detectives.

In addition, this secretive Scorpio Moon opposes Mercury, an astrological indication of deception. The sign on the tenth house also shows the mother; here it is Virgo, ruled by Mercury, so both of her rulers Moon and Mercury, are in conflict. The mother's role in this event is suspicious. Twenty-six degrees of Virgo on the mother's tenth house show a degree of desperation. Mercury also rules the seventh house of the criminal, the "open enemy." Detectives believed that the mother was not completely forthcoming about her little boy's abduction and murder, and the planets reflect this in the event chart. In addition, the Moon-Mercury opposition is in square aspect to Saturn, showing obstruction and detachment.

Mars, ruler of fifth of children, also rules twelfth of secrecy and hidden misdeeds and it finds itself in the critical last degrees of the sign Cancer [family] in the eighth house of death. Was the death a family misdeed, and covered up? We won't know. The mother, who has steadfastly denied any involvement, eventually moved away. Some speculated that she had a boyfriend who may have been involved. For the sake of inquiry, let's examine that angle.

The boyfriend would be the fifth house from the tenth of the mother, or the second in this crime horoscope. The second house is occupied by a Uranus-Neptune conjunction in Capricorn. This describes a volatile, untrustworthy person. The ruler of the boyfriend is Saturn, also in this house, which shows an element of self-interest. Most noticeable is that Saturn is in opposition to Jupiter, Jimmy's ruler, and in square to the Moon. These placements indicate tension and conflict between the three and indicate that Jimmy faced danger from both parties.

Jimmy's remains were eventually found in a wooded area two miles from his home. The manner of death was never determined due to the poor condition of the remains, but the chart suggests possible involvement by the mother and boyfriend. In the next chart of the disappearance and death of another little boy, Tom, the chart will again suggest that the mother's live-in boyfriend was involved in the child's death. This time, justice will be served.

Jimmy

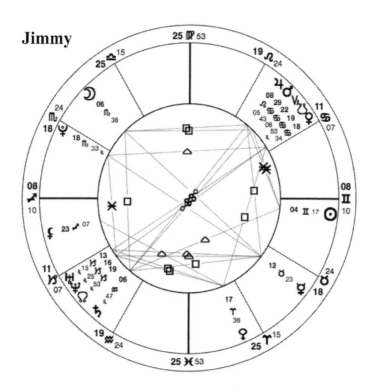

Tom

This was the disturbing case of a six-year-old boy, Tom, who disappeared while under the care of his mother's boyfriend, who later reported him missing. The boyfriend had a violent criminal record and the boy was allegedly afraid of him, but I kept an open mind when working on the horoscope, which I cast using the time he was last seen.

Little Tom is shown by the 16 degrees Aries Ascendant with its ruler Mars in fun-loving Leo in the fifth house. He reportedly had gone out to play in the snow and that was the last time he was seen. Mars is peregrine and opposite Jupiter so there was little or no supervision and the little boy could have wandered off. However, Mars also opposes the Jupiter-Neptune pairing. The opposition usually indicates another person, and a Mars-Neptune opposition often indicates a kidnapping, as we have already seen in the case of baby Lindbergh.

As we have seen in the Lindbergh case and the case of Jean, Mars also rules the eighth house of death (Scorpio) so the child's fate is unfortunate. Mars is peregrine in this degree of Leo. A peregrine planet has no sense of direction and so is vulnerable to outside influences. He is unable to help himself, and with opposition to Jupiter and Neptune, he disappears.

In an abduction the seventh ruler describes the abductor. Here it is Venus, which trines Tom's Mars, showing some affinity or connection between the boy and his abductor. This is where the horoscope gets really interesting. The Moon, Sun and Venus are all ruled by Jupiter, which also rules the twelfth house of convicts. Tom's ruler Mars is in the term and face of Jupiter; he was in the boyfriend's charge, and afraid of the boyfriend. How did I arrive at this?

The mother's boyfriend is the fifth from the tenth house which is ruled by Venus. Venus also rules the seventh house of the perpetrator, the "open enemy." The Moon, which also rules the mother, applies to Venus in Sagittarius by conjunction, showing the connection between the two.

Tragically, little Tom's body was found in a lot near the home. A few weeks later the boyfriend confessed to the killing. In my first analysis of this chart I believed the horoscope suggested a watery death by drowning. Tom lived near a lake so drowning or being disposed of in the lake was a possibility. The fourth house end of the matter is Cancer, the eighth house of death has Scorpio, a water sign, on its cusp, and the Part of Fortune is in the watery sign Pisces. But the lake near the boy's home was searched without success. However, when spring came, the snows melted and the body of the child was found. He had been killed outside and buried in a deep snowdrift. Ironically, he was in a form of water, but not the lake, as I had originally thought.

The horoscope suggests that the mother (Saturn in Libra in the sixth) had some problems with her son, as Mars and Saturn are in negative mutual reception. The Moon also rules the mother, which is peregrine in Sagittarius in the eighth. While she had no involvement in her son's disappearance, the planets suggest an inability to care for him as she may have wished. Her boyfriend, who had initially been charged with negligence in the disappearance, eventually confessed to the crime, so she paid a terrible price for leaving her only child in his care.

Tom

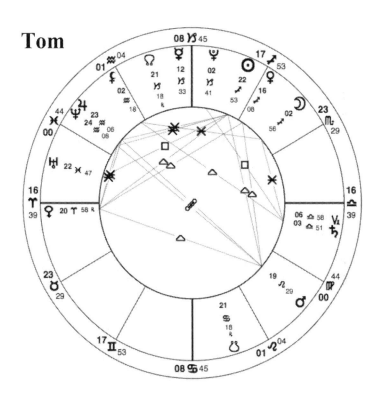

Bob

Medical astrology is a specialized branch of astrology which was used extensively by classical astrologers to diagnose and treat illness. As in conventional astrology, the luminaries, planets and signs represent the organs and parts of the body, and depending on their placement, much information can be gleaned about the condition of a person's health.

In this case, a 12-year-old boy, Bob, was found dead of unknown causes on a city street. I cast the horoscope for the time he was found. He bore no external evidence of gunshot, battery or stab wounds, so I hoped to rely on medical astrology to learn from the planets just what happened to him. In the event horoscope he is shown by 27 degrees Pisces rising.

Late degrees often show something coming to an end. His ruler Jupiter is in the twelfth house of sorrow conjunct Neptune, spelling out a mysterious event which was perhaps covered up – so I thought, maybe a hit and run? The boy was found with some bruising on his body so he apparently suffered some devastating injury while walking along which caused his sudden death. But his skull was intact, so he was not struck by falling debris, and no wounds were found aside from the bruising on his torso.

His planet Jupiter is opposite violent Mars in the sixth house of accidents. This confirms he was involved in a fatal accident. But who and what caused it? The sign of a perpetrator is the seventh house cusp or Descendant. Here it is ruled by Mercury which also rules the third house. Something or someone in transit caused this fatal accident. However, bruising on the body was not significant enough to suggest being struck by a car, and he had no broken bones.

Bob's death was a mystery for several days. Fortunately a witness later came forward to say that he had heard and seen a motorcycle speeding up the street before the boy's body was found. CCTV footage obtained by the police confirmed that a motorcycle had sped down the street just minutes before Bob was found. Moon applying to Uranus in the twelfth describes a sudden accident, which is covered up – it was in fact a hit-and-run.

The autopsy revealed that the cause of death was a lacerated liver, which is borne out by the astrological configurations. In the event chart Jupiter, which rules the liver, was fatally afflicted. Mars, in the sixth, describes an accident. In medical astrology the sixth house also refers to the midsection of the body level with the stomach, liver and digestive organs, which is the approximate area that Bob was struck. Again, the horoscope has reflected the course of events in describing the nature Bob's tragic accident and death.

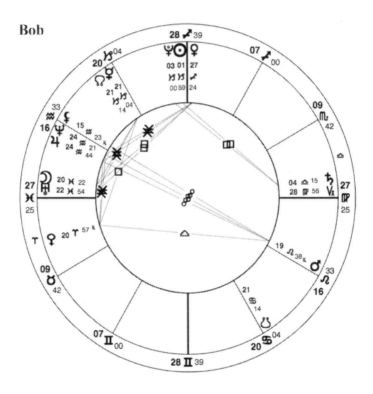

Bob

BRIAN

Missing children are not the only mysteries that I try to solve with the help of forensic horocopes. Often, a startling event in the news, such as an untimely death, captures my attention and I try to figure out what astrological influences were behind the event. Such was my response to the untimely and tragic death of a young musician whom I'll call Brian, whose career was just beginning to show promise when he died of complications resulting from prescription drugs in his Connecticut apartment. I cast the horoscope for the time he was found by his roommate. He was unconscious by then, and prescription drugs were found near the bedside.

Brian is shown by the 5 degrees Cancer Ascendant, its ruler Moon, and also by the natural ruler of artists, Venus. The Moon here is in the second house, in the sign of dramatic Leo. It occupies the exact degree of the Part of Peril, which needs no explanation. Just hours earlier, there had been a Full Moon at 2 degrees Aquarius from this second house to the eighth house of death. The second house concerns matters which are unforeseen – how could he know that the prescription drugs he mixed on that day would prove fatal?

During a Full Moon the light of the Moon reaches its peak illumination, and after waxing full the Moon's light slowly begins to wane. This culmination can signify a crisis, and statistics reveal that emergency rooms, firehouses and police stations report far more activity during a Full Moon than at any other time of the month. It is a critical time, and energies are heightened more than usual, sometimes tending to excessive or extreme actions.

This Moon is in the triplicity of the Sun and the terms of Saturn, both planets being connected to the eighth house of death. Saturn, ruling the eighth of death, is conjunct the cusp of the fourth house, signifying the end of a matter. The chart is describing a fatal tragedy. Brian's other ruler is Venus, which rules the fifth house of entertainment, and also rules actors. This casts more light on his actions: Venus occupies late degrees of Sagittarius, a critical placement, and Venus here is conjunct Pluto, a planet of irreversible damage, in the sixth house of accidents and illnesses. The autopsy revealed that Brian had four prescription drugs in his system, including painkillers and sleep-inducing drugs. Venus also rules the twelfth house of self-undoing; he overmedicated himself and his body could not tolerate the mixture of drugs in his system. Mars, ruler of the sixth house of illness and accidents, is opposite the Venus/Pluto combination from the twelfth house to the sixth: his attempt to overcome illness led to a fatal accident.

After Brian's death it was rumored that he had a substance abuse problem. Confusion surrounding the event is shown in the event chart: ruler of fourth of ending of the matter, Mercury, is conjunct Neptune. The rumors were given mileage by the media, but many were confusing and unclear, which is the mark of a Mercury-Neptune combination. Uranus, at the midheaven, is a testament to the shockwaves felt in his community when the news broke of his premature death. It also reinforces my feeling that the death was indeed accidental, and not a deliberate suicide.

I believe the chart has told us that a tragic misjudgment on this day caused the death of a gifted but fated rising star. This Full Moon, which rose so brightly and as quickly began to lose its brilliance, paid homage to Brian's tragically short-lived musical career.

Brian

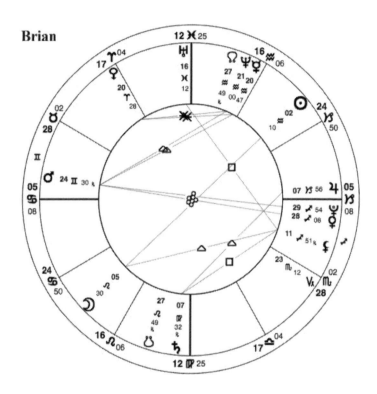

SUSAN

The body of Susan, a college junior, was found in an unresponsive state in her dormitory, where she later died. Authorities ruled out foul play, so I cast a horoscope for the time she was found by her roommate to find out more about this sad incident. Capricorn is the rising sign in this chart, so Susan is represented by its ruler, Saturn. Saturn has just entered both the sign Libra and the ninth house. This describes the fact that she had recently returned to university classes (ninth) and that she was found in the dormitory (also ninth).

Saturn is exalted in Libra and is ruled by Venus: Susan was a very promising student, attractive, popular and well-liked by her peers. With Saturn in its exaltation, triplicity and term, she had great potential for success, and was extremely confident and ambitious. But her strong self-confidence may have led her to a fatal mistake, as the rest of the chart shows. Saturn is afflicted by Pluto in the twelfth house of self-undoing and Saturn disposits Pluto: something Susan did led somehow to her sudden demise.

The Moon in Aries is conjunct the fourth house of endings and receives Saturn (Susan) in its fall, also describing an action with a fatal effect. Venus, also in Libra, separates from Saturn and rules the fifth of recreation. I believe Susan may have attended a party prior to her death and had an encounter with someone there (Moon has also separated from hard aspect to Venus).

I looked to the sixth house of illness to find the source of the fatality. It is ruled by Mercury which is fast approaching combustion to the Sun in Scorpio. Combustion of a planet to the Sun literally destroys the planet's life force and in this case, something affected Susan's health very quickly and ended up killing her. The Sun rules the eighth of death and it also rules the heart. Mars rules the Aries Moon. Since Mars also rules the Moon, and the Moon rules drugs, I believe that she used a recreational or prescription drug that ended up causing cardiac arrest. The interplay between Sun, Moon and Mars describe a very sudden health crisis ending in death.

The toxicology results confirmed the cause of death as accidental death by multiple drug toxicity.

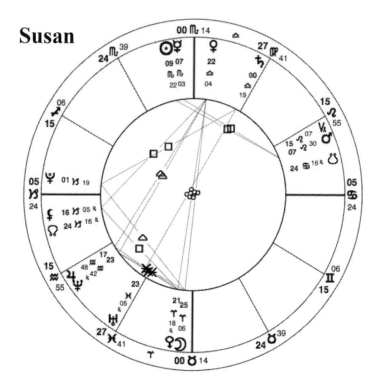

John

On a chilly autumn morning the body of John, a 17-year-old freshman, was found on a college campus. He had leapt to his death from the roof of a building. John had expressed to friends he had been going through a depression, but what could have motivated him to take this final and irreversible step?

In this chart Venus is rising in Libra: John was attractive, charming and personable and he was well-liked by his friends. But a strong Libran facade will want to suppress ugly feelings. And the sign Libra is the detriment of Mars: he would have had trouble venting his anger outwardly and would have struggled with difficult emotions. Venus also rules the eighth house of death, which is never a favorable indication in event charts of this nature.

The beautiful Venus gives more clues to his despondency: it is the exaltation sign of Saturn, in the twelfth house of self-undoing. Saturn forms a challenge aspect to Pluto: in the weeks prior to the suicide he had become increasingly obsessed with his own death. His mental state was degenerating: Mercury approaches combustion to the Sun. Both these planets are entering the second house of self-esteem. His friends described him as likable but lacking in confidence. Venus rising is just separating from a trine to fifth-house Neptune. These aspects suggest that may have recently had a romantic fantasy which led to sudden disappointment for John. I believe his sexuality was also a source of concern: Saturn, ruling fifth house of pleasure, finds itself in the twelfth house of secrecy and sorrow.

Like many Librans, this sensitive student struggled in his relationships with others. Although he had been admired by friends, he admitted to deep feelings of loneliness. The ruler of his fifth house of pleasure and romance was Saturn, occupying the dark twelfth house of suffering and self-undoing. Mars, ruler of seventh of relationships, challenges Mercury/Sun in the first house of self. Unable to cope with the sense of isolation he felt from others, and being unable (in his own mind) to manage his relationships, fascination turned to self-destruction. In order to make his fatal jump from the campus building, John had had to scale several flights of stairs. Only in death was he finally able to express and release the turmoil of his darker side.

In astrology, connections with the twelfth house ruler, regardless of whether it is a commonly thought-of benefic such as Venus, or the malefic Saturn, often factor into suicide, especially when in difficult aspect to Saturn. Following is the case of Karen, an aspiring artist who was found deceased shortly after suffering from a brief illness.

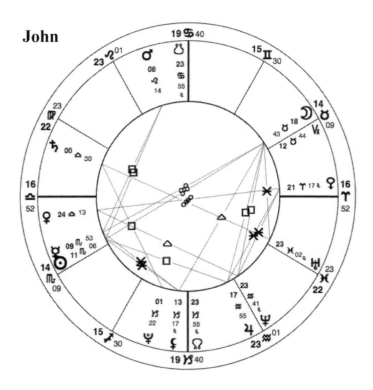

KAREN

In the case of Karen, an attractive model, Neptune is rising at 24 degrees Aquarius which is in exact conjunction with both Jupiter and the Ascendant. Jupiter conjunct Neptune can indicate going overboard with illegal or prescription drugs. Neptune and Jupiter rising, opposite a brash sixth house Mars, describe the potential for accidental misuse of drugs. Jupiter ruling the tenth house shows that this sad incident received media attention. Neptune rising can also denote a celebrity, with the opposition to Mars describing a dangerous act with harmful consequences.

There are other stressful signs in the chart: the Ascendant ruler Saturn is just inside the eighth house, in exaltation, triplicity and terms of itself. Saturn rules the twelfth and first houses. The twelfth house rules hospitals, secrecy and sorrow, and is also the house of self-undoing. The association of Saturn and the twelfth house can be indicative of suicide, whether deliberately carried out with that purpose in mind, or self-undoing caused by confusion and disorientation.

Her ruler Saturn also squares Pluto in the eleventh: her goals and aspirations had something to do with the cause of her death. She had had plastic surgery to improve her appearance but had relied on prescription painkillers afterward. The sixth house Mars indicates an infection or inflammation, for which she was also self-medicating. The medication for the post-surgical pain, mixed with other meds, may have led to her unfortunate early demise.

The afflicted Moon, ruler of the sixth house, approaching sextile with afflicted Saturn, ruler of eighth, shows that her health was already compromised and in a weakened state. Mars in the sixth can describe inflammation or infection of some kind, which weakened her and led to her taking more drugs to combat it. The eighth ruler Venus is also in the term and face of Saturn, her ruler. Ruler of sixth, Moon in Aquarius, is in the twelfth house of self-undoing. The worst houses of the horoscope for illness, the sixth, eighth and twelfth, feature very strongly in this reading.

Several weeks after her passing the coroner ruled that death resulted from multiple drug toxicity and pulmonary infection. While many believed that this was just another accidental overdose, the horoscope bears testimony that Karen was in fact very ill and had relied too heavily on dangerous drug combinations in an ill-fated effort to recover.

Karen

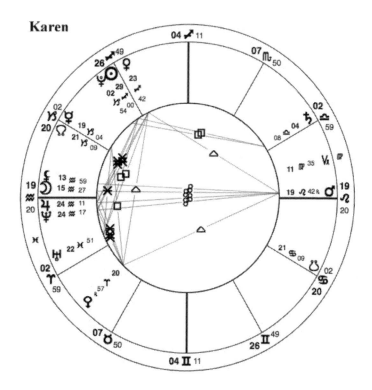

CARL

When twenty-eight-year-old artist Carl passed away suddenly, his friends immediately thought it was the result of suicide by drug overdose. I cast a chart for the time the police were called to see whether any other factors were in play, as in Karen's case.

Three degrees Aquarius is rising with its ruler Saturn retrograde in the eighth house of death. Saturn also rules the twelfth house of self-undoing and sorrow – how often do I see this in cases of this type. Saturn going retrograde in Venus' sign: he was reevaluating relationships, not only romantic, but with the world at large. He was concerned about his earnings: Mercury, ruler of others' resources, was exactly on his second house cusp. Mercury was in detriment, and strongly combust the Sun. He was having financial concerns. Mercury also ruled the fifth house of recreation, so he may have overspent his money on partying and recreational things.

Mars rules his third house of communication and thought. It is retrograde, but stationing, conjunct the Leo seventh house cusp. He felt he was losing some control over business and/or personal relationships. Mars also rules the tenth of career, and in opposition to Carl's Ascendant; this too was a source of conflict and concern. Mars appears to sextile Saturn but this kind of sextile is not helpful; the two planets are in negative mutual reception. Whatever Carl did to solve his issues only made them worse, with the overdose being the final misguided act. At the time of his death he was in fact lonely, unemployed and worried about his future prospects.

The Moon is in its detriment in the twelfth house. It speaks of pained emotions and a sense of being trapped in them, suffering in silence, disillusionment. It is conjunct the Moon's North Node which is unfortunately placed. The Sun in Pisces is also in the same degree as the Moon's nodes, signifying a fateful ending. Carl was not in full control of himself emotionally when he overdosed. He was seeking a mellowed-out, peaceful release from his anxieties.

Sadly for him, and the rest of us, his release was permanent. After reviewing the chart of his final act, I came to agree with his friends that he had in fact taken his own life. The placements of Saturn retrograde in the eighth house, and ruling the twelfth, and in negative relationship to Mars, are indicative of self-undoing.

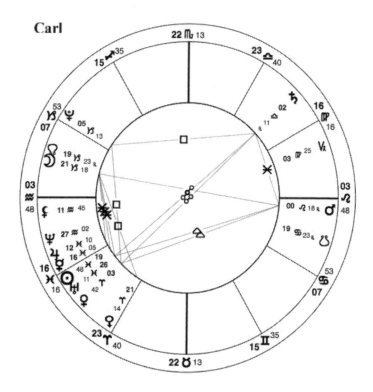

DAVID

A popular young artist, David, was found dead of unknown causes in his Brooklyn apartment. I cast an astrology horoscope for this time to try and understand the circumstances surrounding his unfortunate premature death.

In an event chart the individual inquired about is shown by the Ascendant or first house and its ruling planet. Capricorn was rising and its ruler, Saturn, was at 22 degrees Virgo in the eighth house. As noted in other cases, 22 degrees is an unfortunate placement and it is conjoined to the fixed star Denebola, indicative of destruction and disaster.

Both placements are testimony to a death. The eighth house, as well as Saturn, rules death, and 29 degrees Leo on this house are critical, showing it was too late to effect any change in the matter. Twenty-nine degrees Leo is also the placement of the fixed star Regulus, which signifies a tragic event, one which may command a great deal of publicity.

The planets also show that David was not in a good frame of mind on this day. The Moon is entering the twelfth house of sorrow and self-undoing. Mars in the sixth house of sickness and accidents has just completed opposition to twelfth house Pluto. Mars is also in Cancer, the sign of its fall. Mercury in Libra is square to Mars in the unfortunate sixth house; his thinking and behavior were impulsive, with fatal consequences.

The chart has Venus in Leo in the seventh house, which separates from conjunction with the South Node, another unfortunate star placement showing loss. He had a love interest which had ended recently, and the chart shows he still held onto some attachment to this person. Since Venus is in Leo I believe she was an artist, performer or creative person of some kind.

Drug paraphernalia was found near David's body, and the coroner's ruling was death by accidental drug overdose.

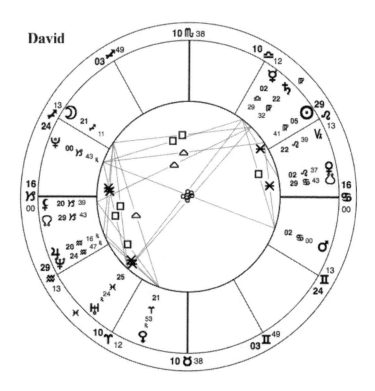

David

Couple

On a fall morning the bodies of a man and a woman were found in a school playground. I cast the astrology chart for the time the bodies were found.

The chart presents an immediate challenge. The couple was reportedly found exactly at 8:00 AM. If the time were off by only four minutes, the Ascendant and house cusps would change. Usually that doesn't pose much of a problem, but here four minutes looms large, because it might shift the Ascendant from 0 Libra to 29 Virgo or even earlier. It would change the Midheaven too, thus affecting all four angles, which as we have seen, are extremely important in any horoscope. However, everything happens for a reason, so I just went with the given time and it yielded a lot of valuable information about this case.

There is something really disturbing about this chart, and it is that the four angles all show the degree of zero. Zero degree of any cardinal sign—Aries, Cancer, Libra, or Capricorn—is considered critical. In this case the fact that two dead bodies turned up in a school playground is certainly a crisis. Something went very wrong in the early morning hours of that day. Zero degrees of Aries is also called "Aries point," and can itself indicate a crisis. Here we have "Aries point" plus three other critical points forming the angles of this event chart.

The Part of Fortune is at 7 degrees Capricorn in the fourth house of endings, disposited by Saturn which is in the twelfth of sorrow and misfortune. What was the couple doing in the playground that night? The couple is shown by the Ascendant ruler which is Venus, occupying 19 degrees Leo in the eleventh house. I believe the couple were out having a good time and I wonder if they were trying to buy or sell drugs: their ruler Venus is in fun-loving Leo in the eleventh house of friends, but opposed by a nasty fifth house Jupiter-Neptune conjunction. I wonder if a drug buy or sale went bad. Venus is in its own terms at 19 Leo; they were into enjoying themselves and having a good time.

The killer is shown by the Descendant, which is ruled by Mars in the tenth house in its fall in Cancer. This Mars in Cancer shows someone who is emotionally volatile and who will react with violence. It is in the sign of its fall, where it is unfavorably motivated but also angular, giving it power to act badly. Mars is also in square aspect to the rising Mercury in Libra in the Ascendant, suggesting a quarrel between the parties. Mars is in the terms of Jupiter; maybe the killer thought he was carrying out some warped act of justice by killing the couple.

The couple also had friends who turned out to be enemies: Venus is ruled by the Sun, which is in the twelfth house of hidden enemies. The couple liked their friends (Venus receives Sun)—but Sun receives Venus in its detriment, showing the feeling was not mutual. Some friend of the couple had a hidden agenda. Could this have led to their murder? The opposition to Neptune speaks of deception or betrayal, possibly involving narcotics. Mars rules the eighth house of death, meaning death by gunshot or possibly a stabbing. Saturn rules fourth of endings, which also suggests blunt force trauma or beating.

The news report stated that the victims had been both shot and beaten. There was a lot of rage expressed in these killings. I am concluding that the killings were the result of a sudden burst of violence due to an argument. The horoscope has reflected the brutal and violent end that this couple encountered in a school playground. Although no one has been apprehended for the killing, astrology suggests that the responsible party had a grudge against the couple for personal reasons and took action out of some warped sense of justice.

Couple

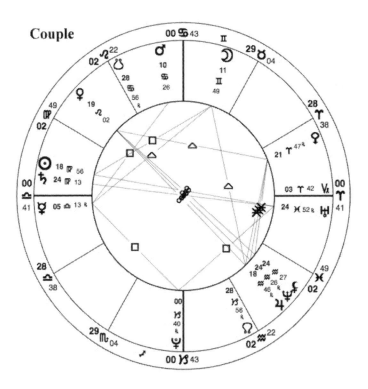

CINDY

The parents of a little girl, whom we'll call Cindy, called police to report her disappearance from her home. As of this writing, some two years later, she has not yet been found.

Unfortunately this event horoscope is not very promising for Cindy. Her ruler Saturn is on the cusp of the eighth house. The Part of Fortune, which describes the outcome of event charts, is elevated at 22 degrees Scorpio in the Midheaven. (The Part of Fortune is not shown in the chart). Its ruler Mars is in its detriment in Taurus on the fourth house cusp of endings. This paints a sad picture with a violent ending. Venus is exalted in Taurus but rules the fourth house of endings and has just contacted Mars before entering the fourth house. Venus in aspect to Mars in a crime chart may suggest a physical attraction that the perpetrator felt for the victim, often not of the victim's choosing, or a sexually based motive for the crime.

Cindy is represented by the Ascendant, 23 Capricorn, and Capricorn is also the sign on the twelfth house cusp of sorrow and suffering. Her ruler, Saturn, is in the eighth house of death. Pluto, on the twelfth house cusp, opposes the sixth house Sun in Cancer, the Sun being the natural ruler of children. The Sun in Cancer in a cadent house is also an unhappy testimony to the fate of the child. The eighth house cusp is 29 degrees of Leo, the natural sign of children, but at 29 degrees, it is too late to help her. Very late degrees also describe a desperate situation, which is clearly shown.

I looked to the seventh house to find out just what kind of creature would abduct and abuse a young innocent girl. The planets are very revealing.

The abductor is ruled by 23 degrees Cancer and I turned the chart so that the seventh house became the Ascendant. First thing I noted was that 23 degrees Cancer is conjunct the evil fixed star Pollux, whom the ancients called "the wicked boy." Castor and Pollux were fraternal twins in Greek mythology; Castor being the girl, and Pollux being the boy, who was trouble-prone and much worse behaved than his sister. The famous German astrologer Reinhold Ebertin-Hoffman described Pollux: "... this star is brutal, tyrannical, violent and cruel if in conjunction with the Lights, Ascendant or Meridian or even linked with malefics."[1] We have already seen this fixed star in the Ascendant of the event chart for the death of Marilyn Monroe.

In this chart, Pollux is the abductor's Ascendant ("Lights" referred to above) and it in fact forms a Grand Trine in water with Uranus in Pisces and the unfortunate Part of Fortune in Scorpio. Pollux has a negative effect in this chart. The Grand Trine shows that the perp gave in to a sudden fit of uncontrolled aggression, leading to a violent ending.

The Moon rules the perp's Ascendant and is located in Virgo, applying to Saturn on the eighth house cusp. The chart had much to say about this particular offender, so I developed a psychological profile based on what the planets described.

This act was deliberate and planned: Saturn and Mercury are in mutual reception and form a square. They are also contra-antiscion each other. This person is capable of extreme concentration on what he set out to do. He is cold and calculating, with obsessive attention to detail. This may not have been his first abduction.

Since feminine signs predominate here, I believe he is somewhat effeminate, and emotionally very insecure, which he tries to make up for by relying on intellectual and organizational skills. He is likely a bachelor (Moon in Virgo), also likely a registered sex offender (Venus/Mars conjunct, square Jupiter/Neptune), and this also suggests he may have a prison record during the past four to five years.

He has the tendency to fantasize that children are his sex partners (ruler of his fifth of children conjunct Neptune/Chiron) and he will go to great lengths to achieve gratification at any cost (Venus/Mars conjunct in Taurus square Jupiter/Neptune). He is anal in his own personal habits and may only be stimulated by small children.

The perpetrator has the Moon ruling both his Ascendant and twelfth house, so he is his own worst enemy. Someone like this eventually gets careless and does himself in or ends up getting caught. We can only hope.

This example illustrates the use of astrology in drawing a criminal profile for the offender. I believe the planets can help us discern valuable information about events and those who participate in them. If members of law enforcement took notice of the value of astrology in gathering such valuable information, it would be extremely useful in finding out critical information that is often lacking in cold cases.

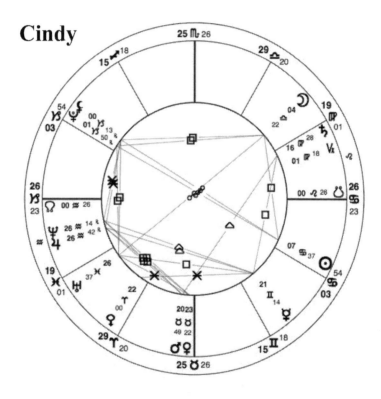

Cindy

Endnotes

1 Ebertin-Hoffman, *op. cit.*, 41.

CHAPTER FOUR

Natural and Unnatural Disasters

So far we have seen how astrology can help to explain the circumstances surrounding missing persons, accidents and murders. It is also very useful when applied to natural disasters such as earthquakes, and unnatural disasters, such as plane crashes and shipwrecks. Ancient astrologers relied heavily on eclipses and the positions of the fixed stars when choosing the safest times for long-distance travel. As with any event, there were good times to embark upon journeys, and bad times.

In fact, centuries ago it was customary for the royal courts of Europe and the Middle East to consult astrologers for the best times to conduct important business: when to marry, when to crown a new ruler and even when to wage war. In order to make these determinations the astrologers would gather information from heavenly events. The movements of the planets, positions of the stars and eclipses of the Sun and Moon were commonly used methods. Astrologers of the day understood that whatever happened on earth was also reflected in the movements of the heavens. There were several rules of thumb that they followed in selecting good times for events to take place. Most notable among these were the quality of the Ascendant and Moon and their rulers; if travel were involved look also to Mercury, and none of the ruling planets should be in harsh aspect to the malefics.

The two aviation accidents, the earthquake, and the ill-fated cruise discussed here all show a strong degree of difficulty with regard to the Ascendant, the placement and quality of its ruler, and the quality of the Moon and its ruler. The positions of the fixed stars, as well as eclipses preceding some of these events, also foreshadowed grave danger.

The Crash of TWA Flight 800

There are many factors to take into consideration when studying an event chart. In addition to the positions of the planets and eclipses preceding the event, the placements of the fixed stars and the Arabic Parts or Lots of Fortune are also revealing. Often these give a wealth of information on their own and can be eerily accurate in describing the situation.

On July 17, 1996, a TWA Boeing 747 jet airliner took off from JFK Airport in Long Island. The 230 passengers and crew members aboard the flight were destined for Rome with a stopover in Paris. But within fifteen minutes of take-off, their destiny took a tragic twist, and on that night TWA Flight 800 became the third deadliest air accident to occur in U.S. history.[1] The incident was especially sad because sixteen passengers were high-school students from Montoursville, Pennsylvania, who as members of their high school French Club had just embarked on their first trip to Paris. What does the event chart for this terrible disaster reveal?

The event chart portrays a disturbing picture with many dangerous energies coming into play within minutes of the take-off. The Ascendant is zero degrees Aquarius, a critical degree, and Uranus, planet which signifies the unpredictable and often shocking, is on the Ascendant. It is in conjunction with the fixed star Altair in the Aquila constellation known as "the Flying Eagle." When configured with malefics, the fixed stars often signify catastrophic events. Witnesses reported that the aircraft suddenly exploded and crashed into the water. An explosion is aptly described by Uranus rising. The Ascendant and Uranus were also in opposition to Mercury, the planet which rules travel. In his *Complete Dictionary of Astrology* Alan Leo states of the travel planet: "… let Mercury be free from combustion and evil aspects of the infortunes …for such an election denotes safety, joy and gladness in the journey."[2]

Sadly, this was not the case. Mercury is separating from combustion with Sun, but is still within eight degrees, so it is "under the sunbeams." It is peregrine, meaning that it has no essential dignity in the third degree of Leo, and it is afflicted by Uranus, planet of accidents. It is also in trine aspect to Pluto in Sagittarius, which rules long-distance journeys. A trine between weakened planets does not bode much better for the flight than the harder aspects; sometimes it indicates that dangerous incidents can happen with ease.

Jupiter, which rules long-distance travel, is also badly aspected: it is in Capricorn, its sign of fall, in the twelfth house of sorrow and secrecy. It is at eleven degrees, the same degree as the Moon's lunar nodes. A planet in the same degree of the lunar nodes is a harbinger of fate. These combined energies suggest an unfortunate outcome.

As the Ascendant ruler, Saturn rules the aircraft in this chart, and it also is badly placed in Aries where it cannot function. Saturn in Mars' territory is very unfortunate: both planets are considered as malefics and signify great danger. The jet was barely able to remain airborne for fifteen minutes before it exploded and crashed. Another difficult indication in a flight horoscope is when the Ascendant ruler also rules the eighth or twelfth houses. Here, Saturn also rules the twelfth house of cover-ups and secret enemies. The unusual and sudden explosion of the plane, and the differing accounts by eyewitnesses, who were questioned only once by the authorities and not asked to review or verify their statements, gave rise to conspiracy theories that the plane had been shot down by a missile or was otherwise the subject of a terrorist act.[3] Some witnesses claimed they had seen a flash streaking toward the plane, which then exploded into two parts and crashed. Others heard an explosion. After extensive investigation, the official cause of the crash was given as an explosion in the fuel tank, causing vapors to ignite and explode. The official NTSB ruling was "explosion of center wing fuel tank resulting from ignition of the flammable fuel/air mixture in the tank."[4]

However, some aspects of the event chart introduce the possibility of something secretive about this occurrence. By its rulership of both the twelfth and first houses Saturn rules both the aircraft and secret enemies. Open enemies are ruled by the Sun, ruler of the seventh house sign, Leo. Here the Sun is in tight opposition to Neptune, in the twelfth house. Was some deception at work here? The Sun, and Saturn, are in mixed mutual reception, suggesting some parties in collusion with each other. Many believe the entire truth about the crash of TWA Flight 800 will never be revealed, and often the investigators of major incidents do not give the entire truth to the public for reasons of national security, or for politically motivated reasons.

Along with Altair rising at the time of take-off, the fixed star Algenib was also rising as this tragic incident unfolded. The fixed star Algenib is located in the constellation Pegasus, the Winged Horse. This star is in the nature of Mercury, ruling travel, and Mars, ruling violence. If configured to Saturn, there is difficulty and obstruction. Here, the star is configured to Uranus, and the flight barely reached altitude before it exploded and crashed in a fiery blaze.

At the I.C. of the chart, its fourth house cusp, is the star considered the most malefic of fixed stars, Algol. The name Algol comes from the Arabic, "Al Ghoul," meaning devil, evil spirit or demon.[5] Algol is most often indicative of violence, tragedy and death, and it is exactly on the cusp of the fourth house, end of the matter. By all indications, the weak placements of the ruling planets and the positions of the fixed stars set a course of most unfortunate destiny for TWA Flight 800.

TWA Flight 800

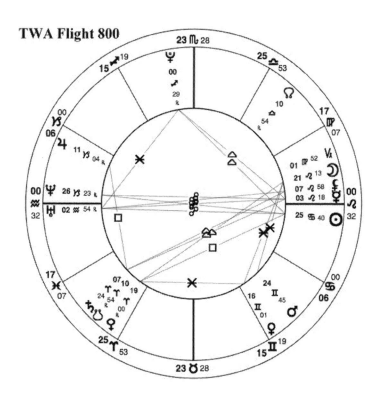

ENDNOTES

1 TWA Flight 800, http://www.wikipedia.org/wiki/TWA_Flight_800.

2 Leo, Alan. *Dictionary of Astrology*, (Montana: Kessinger Publishing, 2003) 224.

3 http://www.flight800.org.

4 Aircraft Accident Report, NTSB Number AAR-00/03, http://www.ntsb.gov.

5 Ebertin-Hoffman, *op.cit.*, 24.

The Strange Descent
of the Air France Airbus

On the night of May 31, 2009, an Air France jet bound for Paris from Rio de Janeiro, Brazil went missing over the Atlantic Ocean. At 2:14 AM UTC (universal time) the flight data recordings stopped, signaling an electrical failure. The jet then stalled and went into free-fall, descending vertically until it plunged into the ocean. Its remains were found scattered for miles from the site of its descent into the ocean.[1]

I used the time of take-off, 7:03 PM BZT, for the event horoscope. If we compare the configuration of the planets in the following horoscope to Alan Leo's rules for a safe journey cited in his *Dictionary of Astrology*, we will find ample reason that the Air France Flight #447 was destined for a tragic ending.

Leo says:

"In the beginning of any journey let the Moon be increasing in light and motion, free from impediment and affliction of the infortunes, for an infortune afflicting the Moon does more hurt than when it afflicts the Ascendant, and let her not be in the second, eighth, fourth, sixth, nor twelfth, but in the fifth, and if possible beheld of the fortunes."[2]

In the event horoscope the Moon, cadent in the ninth house, separates from conjunction with Saturn in the ninth house of long-distance travel and it is in Saturn's terms. It is opposite Uranus on the cusp of the fourth house of endings. Its dispositor, Mercury, is also peregrine. This Moon is increasing in light, but otherwise is afflicted and not in good aspect with any fortunate planet.

Now we check the status of Mercury, planet ruling travel:

"Also let Mercury be free from combustion and evil aspects of the infortunes; place also a fortune in the Ascendant or an angle, for such an election denotes safety, joy and gladness in the journey...."[3] Here Mercury is free from combustion but trines an afflicted Moon and squares an exact conjunction of Jupiter and Neptune on the cusp of the third house of travel. Malefics Uranus and Pluto are angular, and the only fortune angular is Venus, which is in detriment in Aries. The indications for the success of Flight #447 are not favorable.

There was initially a great deal of disagreement among engineers and scientists as to the exact fate of the Airbus. Did the plane explode in midair, or break apart in midair before it fell into the ocean? Was it an act of terrorism? What does the event horoscope have to say about the deadliest accident in the history of the Air France airline?[4]

The angles also tell a disturbing story. In the chart cast for take-off time, Pluto, planet of destruction, is rising, and unpredictable Uranus is on the fourth house cusp of endings. Pisces, a water sign on the fourth house, also rules the ocean, the jet's final resting place.

The violent fixed star Denebola is at the midpoint between the Moon and the Midheaven. Denebola is of the nature of Uranus, Venus and Saturn and is located at 22 degrees Virgo. By the time of the air disaster, some three hours and forty-five minutes after take-off, the Moon had advanced to conjunction with this dangerous star. The early Twentieth Century astrologer W.J. Simmonite, in his *Arcana of Astrology*, writes that Denebola signifies "misfortunes from water and vehicles of conveyance."[5] We will see Denebola appear later on in another massive sea disaster. So far, the planetary and angular configurations describe extreme danger.

I also calculated the Part of Plane Crash, an Arabic part devised by astrologer Priscilla Gilbert in her book, *Potential Fulfilled: Accident Patterns, Vol. I.*[6] This Part is obtained by adding the degrees of the Ascendant to the degrees on the ninth cusp, and subtracting Pluto. The Part of Plane Crash is 23 degrees Leo and is conjunct the cusp of the ninth house of long-distance travel.

I also considered the overall health of the plane, which we know was faulty. The health of a person or object is shown by the Ascendant and the first house, not the sixth as commonly taught in modern astrology. The Ascendant here is Capricorn, and Pluto, a planet of mass annihilation, is conjoined to it. Mars at zero degrees Taurus in the fifth house trines Pluto. Mars is in its detriment so the trine facilitates failure through inability to take effective action. And Mars has just entered Taurus, so it has lost much of its power by exiting its sign of rulership and entering its sign of debility. A planet in a zero degree has just changed energies, sometimes for the worst. See the Appendix for more on critical degrees of signs.

In ancient astrology Mars was also considered ruler of the captain of a ship, and here it rules the pilot. The investigation revealed that the pilot was not properly trained to deal with the malfunction of the altitude alert system.[7] Mars in Taurus, as we have seen, has just gone from its ruled sign Aries, a position of strength, to its sign of fall, Taurus, where it is sluggish and ineffective. The final investigation placed a great deal of the blame for this catastrophe squarely on pilot error.[7] Mars is also in trine to Pluto, so the consequences of this weakness resulted in total devastation.

Saturn, ruler of the Ascendant, is weak: it is cadent in the ninth house, and peregrine. It is conjunct the Moon in Virgo, which rules both the seventh house of passengers and the eighth of death. The Moon is applying to opposition with Uranus, foreshadowing a sudden violent end. Something was amiss in the plane's systems, and with Mercury, planet of communication and travel, as ruler and term ruler of Saturn, it is most likely to do with electronics and communication.

At 11:14 PM the final signal went out from the Air France Airbus reporting an electrical failure, and minutes later the plane fell straight down at high speed to its watery grave. At that moment the Moon had just entered exact conjunction with the violent fixed star Denebola. This conjunction occurred at the fateful point of 22 degrees Virgo, which was the Midheaven point when the plane took off. It describes a vehicular disaster which captured world attention (tenth house).

Foreshadowings of disaster are often given by solar or lunar eclipses preceding the event. In this case, a lunar Full Moon eclipse took place on February 9, 2009, at 23 degrees Leo, which is conjunct both the part of Plane Crash and the cusp of the ninth house of travel in this event chart. Interactions between malefic planets, fixed stars, critical degrees and eclipse points can all signal a devastating event. The crash of the Airbus is still under investigation, but the planets have already told their grim story.

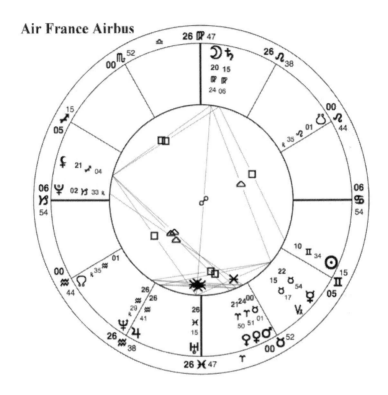

Air France Airbus

ENDNOTES

1 Air France 447, http://www.wikipedia.org/wiki/Air_France_447.

2 Leo, Alan., *Dictionary of Astrology*, (Montana: Kessinger Publishing, 2003), 57.

3 *Ibid.*

4 Air France 447, http://www.wikipedia.org/wiki/Air_France_447

5 Simmonite, W.J. *Arcana of Astrology*, (North Hollywood: Symbols & Signs, 1977), 172.

6 Gilbert, Priscilla M. *Potential Fulfilled: Accident Patterns*, vol. I, (Tempe: American Federation of Astrologers, 1976), 9.

7 "Air France crash blamed on pilot error," http://www.guardian.co.uk/world/2011/jul/29/air-france-crash-pilot-error (July 29, 2011).

THE HAITI EARTHQUAKE

On January 12, 2010, at 4:58 PM local time, the island nation of Haiti was rocked by an earthquake of devastating magnitude, killing hundreds of thousands, destroying thousands of homes and businesses and leaving millions injured and homeless. If Haiti had had a royal astrologer who was familiar with the astrology of the nation and the times, I believe that this disaster could have been foreseen.

A study of the natal horoscope of Haiti and the event and eclipse charts are powerful evidence that astrology can alert us to impending challenges. What do these charts have to say about this tragic event? Let's look first at the birth chart for the potential of future disasters.

Modern day Haiti was formed on January 1, 1804, at 12 noon in the then-capital city of Gonaives.[1] The country is a double Capricorn, with Sun in Capricorn and Capricorn rising. This cardinal earth sign is also occupied by Mars, Mercury and Venus, forming a powerful stellium of planets clustered at the chart's Capricorn Ascendant.

It is interesting that planet Mercury is rising on Haiti's birth Ascendant at 17 degrees of Capricorn. According to early Egyptian astrologer Ptolemy, Mercury ruled earthquakes.[2] Mercury is under stress aspect to Uranus, which is often significant in horoscopes involving accidents and catastrophes. The natal chart of Haiti shows the potential for a disaster of some kind; the island has been victimized by severe hurricanes and earthquakes in the past, and here we see strong reference to the earth element. And Capricorn is as earthy as it gets. But that's not all.

The narrative of astrology is often literal. Several cardinal earth signs teeter at the earth's horizon as if poised to tip over at the slightest push. The quality of this earth element is cold and dry. The earthy triplicity, consisting of Taurus, Virgo and Capricorn is known for its groundedness and stability. By their astrological nature, coldness restricts and contains, and dryness firms and defines boundaries. Yet during an earthquake the opposite occurs. Why such a massive upheaval in earth?

Capricorn is ruled by Saturn, a slow heavy planet of deprivation, hard work, limitations and restrictions. True to this description Haiti has been a country of extremely poor people living in hardscrabble conditions, ruled by a power elite. Saturn, ruler of the chart and so many of its planets, finds itself in its exaltation sign of Libra in the ninth house, suggesting that the well-being of the country comes from foreign sources.

The birth chart describes other stressors in the life of Haiti and its people. Mars is in the twelfth house of sorrows and hidden enemies, forming a tight square to Saturn in the ninth, suggesting a strong military at odds with foreign interests. The Moon is in the eighth house of others' resources and opposes Pluto in the second house of finance and assets, suggesting power struggles with the country's resources.

Several powerful factors came together to trigger this massive calamity on January 12, 2010, and the charts demonstrate this activity. Let's review the chart of the January 12th earthquake, which occurred moments before sunset, placing the sign of Capricorn on the Descendant. Again, there is a preponderance of Capricorn signs: Venus, Sun and the Dragon's Head occupy the seventh house in that sign, while Mercury is retrograde in Capricorn in the sixth house, conjunct Pluto. This time Saturn, ruler of the Ascendant in Haiti's birth chart, rules both the seventh house of relationships and the eighth house of death: the heavy reliance on foreign aid promised in the nativity is now essential to Haiti's recovery. And again Saturn is powerful and influential in the event chart. It is at 4 degrees of Libra, just one degree past its position in the natal chart, 3 degrees Libra. When Saturn returns to the same degree that it occupies in the birth chart it is know as a "Saturn return," a time when the individual is faced with stressful challenges and crises. This Saturn is just past exact square to Pluto, signifying a destruction so massive that complete rebuilding will be required to restore the country to normalcy.

Even in the earthquake chart there is a stellium of planets in the sign Capricorn, once again emphasizing the cold-dry element of firmness and fixity that is destroyed by the earthquake. We also note a cazimi conjunction of the Sun with Venus at 22 degrees Capricorn in the eighth house, which I believe is the key to understanding how the heavens reflect this catastrophe.

The Sun is a powerful force in astrology. Like the real Sun of our solar system, it gives life, but also has the ability to scorch, scald and burn, and so it does with planets that approach it. Planets that come within 17 degrees range of the Sun are considered "under the sunbeams"; they are drained of their own power, like a sunbather who has spent too much time on the beach. Coming even closer to the Sun, within 7 degrees, a planet is considered combust, and becomes even weaker still, too impaired to function efficiently. However, some early astrologers considered that a planet within 16 or 17 minutes of one degree of arc to the Sun is suddenly fortified, and this event is called "cazimi."

The seventeenth century astrologer William Lilly had this to say: "A planet under the beams of Sun, (viz. within 12 degrees), has no fortitude; if within sixteen minutes of Sun, he is in cazimi or heart of Sun, and then he is very strong."[3] In some of my research I've found that the power conferred by a cazimi conjunction was interpreted as a benefic influence. However, in my experience I have yet to see any favorable incident associated with it. As Lilly said, the cazimi was very strong, and in this case, it occurred in a very unfortunate place: the eighth house of death, a literal reference to the fate of Haiti's populace. I believe the cazimi conjunction of Sun-Venus in the earth element was the final energetic trigger for an extreme imbalance in earth energy, enough to cause destruction and death on a catastrophic scale.

The earthquake was also foreshadowed by a penumbral lunar eclipse which took place just six months earlier, on July 7, 2009. As Astrologer Alan Leo said, "Earthquakes generally follow close on the heels of eclipses."[4] This eclipse occurred across the Cancer-Capricorn axis at 16 degrees of Capricorn, which was the degree rising on the Ascendant of the event horoscope at the moment of the earthquake. This point is also in direct opposition to Haiti's natal rising Mercury, at 17 degrees of Capricorn. In fact the axis of this eclipse affected not only the planets in transit on that day but also vital points in the natal chart of Haiti.

As much as we rely today on advanced technology to study the weather, the atmosphere, and to spy on each other, there is no predictive technology in place to keep track of the motions of the planets and to analyze their effect on planet Earth. Such technology would surely have forewarned us of the dangers to Haiti and to other events discussed in this book.

Haiti Earthquake

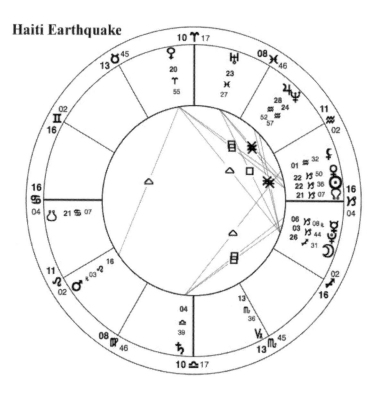

ENDNOTES

1 http://www.marxists.org/history/haiti/1804/liberty-or-death.
htm

2 Lehman, J. Lee. *The Book of Rulerships*, (Westchester: Whitford Press, 1992), 81.

3 Lilly, William. *Introduction to Astrology*, (Delhi: A. Sagar Book House, 1993) 171.

4 Leo, *op. cit.*, 47.

Sinking of the Costa Concordia

Three months prior to the hundred-year anniversary of the tragic sinking of the Titanic, another large cruise ship, the Costa Concordia, sank off the eastern coast of Italy. Many were quick to make comparisons between the two disasters. But who would have known that the sinking of the Costa Concordia followed a pattern first noted in the chart of her unfortunate predecessor?

On the evening of Friday, January 13, 2012, 3,206 passengers and 1,023 crewmen set sail on a Mediterranean cruise aboard the Costa Concordia. Like the Titanic, the Costa was the largest ocean liner in its fleet, costing $569 million to build.[1] Just two and a half hours later, it would strike a shallow reef off the coastline and begin to take in water. At the end, this magnificent liner sank onto its side, where it remained, too dangerous to continue rescue operations. Thirty-two people died, 64 were injured and two were missing and presumed dead. The captain was charged with multiple counts of manslaughter and for weeks afterward the international press was abuzz with reports of negligence and cowardice.

The Costa set sail at 7:30 PM from the western port of Civitavecchia and continued north up the Italian coastline. It was to make six stops in all. However, when approaching the island of Giglio, the captain decided to steer the ship closer to shore so that the inhabitants could view the ship's spectacular light show. It was a dangerous and reckless decision; the ship entered waters far too shallow for its depth, struck a shoal 150 meters from the shoreline and began to sink. It was a scene eerily reminiscent of the Titanic's run-in with the iceberg which damaged several levels of the ship's hull and caused it to slowly capsize. According to witness accounts, the captain and crew were slow to carry out rescue operations and left the ship before all passengers were evacuated to safety. The captain's behavior has since come under harsh scrutiny and the Italian press has had a field day with the disaster.

The ancient astrologers were adept at choosing optimal times for ships to embark on sea travels, and there were certain rules to follow in charting a safe and trouble-free journey. Let's examine some of the rules for safe travel as catalogued in Alan Leo's *Dictionary of Astrology:*

"In the beginning of any journey let the Moon be increasing in light and motion, free from impediment and affliction of the infortunes, for an infortune afflicting the Moon does more hurt than when it afflicts the Ascendant, and let her not be in the second, eighth, fourth, sixth, nor twelfth, but in the fifth, and if possible beheld of the fortunes. Also let Mercury be free from combustion and evil aspects of the infortunes; place also a fortune in the Ascendant or an angle, for such an election denotes safety, joy and gladness in the journey; and let not the Moon be in the Ascendant, neither going nor returning, for it signifies sickness and grief in the journey."[2]

The first test that this travel chart fails is the Moon. Here the Moon is decreasing in light and approaching conjunction with Mars, so it is not free from impediment. The Ascendant is 22 degrees Leo. As we have seen elsewhere, 22 degrees of any sign is problematic. We also have the Descendant is at 22 degrees Aquarius, Mars at 22 degrees Virgo and the Sun at 22 degrees Capricorn, all worrisome energies. The Sun is the Ascendant ruler, in the sixth house of accidents and misfortune, a place where its companion light, the Moon, should never be in a travel chart.

So far the planets are not reflecting an easy, enjoyable cruise. In addition, the Moon rules the twelfth house which is traditionally considered a house of secrecy, confinement and sorrow.

"… and let her [Moon] not be in the second, eighth, fourth, sixth, nor twelfth, but in the fifth, and if possible beheld of the fortunes."[3] Here the troubled Moon is in the second house, another undesirable placement. And it is not beheld, or in aspect, to the fortunes, Venus or Jupiter, which are themselves poorly placed: Venus is at critical 29 degrees Aquarius, exactly conjunct Neptune, and Jupiter is at a critical zero degree of Taurus, where it is peregrine and cadent. The Moon is in trine aspect to the Sun, but the Sun is on the unfortunate sixth house cusp, in square to its dispositor Saturn. This was an ill-fated cruise from the start, which would not reach its destination.

The Sun, chart ruler, in square aspect to Saturn, is especially dangerous. Saturn rules structures. At the end, the ship's structure was decimated, and it was considered a total loss. The troubled Moon here is conjunct Mars, not well placed at 22 degrees Virgo as we have already noted.

In the event chart the ship's hull is shown by the fourth house, and its ruler is the troublesome and violent Mars. In traditional astrology Mars also rules the captain of ships, and I also used the ruler of the tenth house to signify the captain, because he is the leader or "boss" in charge of the cruise.

The chart shows that the captain did not have the ship's best interests at heart. His ruler is Venus, at 29 degrees of Aquarius, a critical placement, and also super conjunct Neptune, with only 13 minutes of arc separating them. (Note: This is not a "cazimi" conjunction, as discussed in the chapter on Haiti. A cazimi conjunction can occur only between a planet and the Sun.) The captain's decision was misguided and impervious to the dangers that lie ahead. Venus and Saturn are in mutual reception by rulership, and are also in trine to each other; his mental error led to disastrous consequences. The captain later tried to blame the entire incident on faulty equipment readings, and claimed to have been among the last to leave the ship, which was contradicted by eyewitnesses who saw him try to leave before the ship's evacuation was complete. With Neptune conjunct his planet Venus, he made a misguided decision and then tried to deny his responsibility in the matter.

I also tracked the progress of the Costa by casting separate event charts for the launch and for the time when the liner first struck the reef, which was approximately 10 PM local time. The resulting charts provide an interesting timeline. At 10 PM the Ascendant has moved to 21 degrees of Virgo, within a degree of conjunction with the fixed star Denebola. In ancient times Denebola was associated with catastrophes at sea, and astrologers would look out for this fixed star when judging charts of important voyages. The afflicted Ascendant, with Denebola at its helm, is also straddled by the Moon-Mars conjunction. Moon and Mars were known to the ancients to activate malefic fixed stars nearby, and this happened exactly when the Costa struck the shallow reef.

And just how does this compare to the demise of the mighty Titanic of one hundred years ago? When the unsinkable ship was launched on April 10, 1912, the fearsome fixed star Denebola was in the event chart of the ship's launch, conjunct the same Ascendant sign and degree as the Costa Concordia. The famous astrologer Ebertin-Hoffman sums it up as follows:

"Denebola was in a conjunct position with the Ascendant, when one of the first giants of the ocean, the TITANIC, was launched."[4] (p. 56) It's no coincidence that so many drew parallels between the Costa Concordia and the Titanic. Even the stars and planets agreed.

Concordia Departure

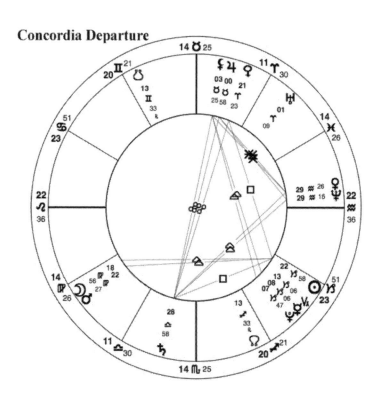

Concordia Sinking

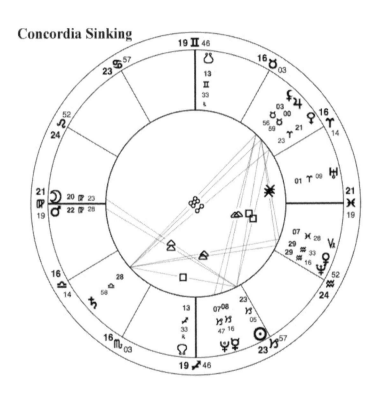

Endnotes

1 Air France, http://www.wiki[edia.org/wiki/Costa_Concordia

2 Leo, *op. cit.*, 57.

3 Leo, *op. cit.*, 57.

4 Ebertin-Hoffman, *op. cit.*, 56.

Appendix

1. Glossary of Astrological Terms

Affliction
A planet is said to be afflicted when it is in a difficult aspect to another planet or when it is poorly placed by essential or accidental dignity. Its energies cannot be expressed easily and are compromised. An example of affliction is Moon in square aspect to Saturn or Venus in opposition to Jupiter.

Air signs
There are three signs belonging to the Air element: Gemini, Libra and Aquarius. The Air signs are inclined toward mental activity, communication and ideas.

Angles, Angular
The angles of the chart are the cusps of the first, fourth, seventh and tenth houses. They define the four quadrants or sections of the horoscope, from houses one through three, houses four through six, houses seven through nine, and houses ten through twelve. Proximity of a planet to an angle confers more power to a planet or star and gives that planet more influence over the affairs of that house.
Example: The seventh house cusp is 20 degrees of Cancer. Mars at 19 degrees of Cancer is on the cusp, it is angular and so has dominion over the seventh house matter. Angularity also gives power to a planet even if it is already inside the house, such as Mars at 25 degrees Cancer in this example.

Antiscion
Two planets which have the same declination on the same side of the equator.

Applying
A planet that is approaching the degree of another planet by aspect.

Examples: Moon at 12 degrees of Taurus applies to a square of Venus at 15 degrees of Leo. The Sun at 17 degrees Libra applies to a conjunction with Saturn at 19 degrees of Libra.

Arabic Parts, or Lots
See also Section 5 of this Appendix. The Arabic Parts, or Lots as they are also called, signify areas of the zodiac found by calculating the distances between house cusps and planets related to specific inquiries. The rulers of these Parts are often of significance in the chart. The Parts were developed in antiquity but are useful even today, and a Part or Lot can be calculated for just about anything by adding and subtracting degrees of planets and cusps on the 360-degree wheel. See Section 5.

Ascendant
Also called "rising sign," the Ascendant is the easternmost point on the horoscope and is the cusp of the first house of the chart. In a person, it represents the physical appearance, health and personality. In an event chart, the Ascendant shows the event in question, and in a crime chart it shows the victim of the crime. The ruler of the Ascendant, its dignities and placement yield a great deal of information in a crime chart of a missing or murdered person.

Aspect
A planet aspects another planet when it forms a relationship by quality, element or triplicity. The main aspects are conjunction, sextile, square, trine and opposition.

Benefic
A helpful or beneficial planet, usually Venus or Jupiter, if well placed in a chart.

Cardinal signs

One of the four qualities of the signs of the zodiac. The cardinal (also called movable) signs are Aries, Cancer, Libra and Capricorn. *See also:* Fixed Signs, Mutable Signs.

Cazimi

When a planet or the Moon is within 17 minutes of arc from the Sun.

Conjunction

When one planet occupies the same sign of another planet within an orb of five degrees or less. Mercury at 13 degrees Taurus approaches conjunction with Mars at 16 degrees Taurus.

Critical degrees - See **Degrees.**

Cusp

A line which divides one house of a horoscope from another, which will always show the degree of a sign.

Degree

See also Section 6 of this Appendix - **Degrees of Danger.**

All horoscopes are 360-degree circles, so one degree is 1/360th of the circle. A degree may or may not be occupied by a planet, star or other celestial body. Ancient astrologers attributed various qualities to specific degrees of the zodiac and these are called "critical degrees."

29 degrees of any sign is considered critical, or fateful, because it denotes something coming to a quick end, something which has been building up and is ready to end or burst. Zero degrees indicates a sudden change in a situation, something new coming to light, or a beginning. Zero degrees of any cardinal sign is referred to as "Aries point," which in modern astrology relates to a public persona of the native, one's place in the world. Critical degrees are often found in the crime charts and event charts of disasters in this book. Other critical degrees are: 4 and 17 of mutable signs

[Gemini, Virgo, Sagittarius, Pisces], 0, 13 and 26 of cardinal signs [Aries, Cancer, Libra, Capricorn], and 8-9 and 21-22 of fixed signs [Taurus, Leo, Scorpio, Aquarius]. 18 and 19 degrees of Aries/ Libra are considered "degrees of homicide" by astrologer Edna Rowland. 22 degrees of any sign are considered as traumatic or fateful, as seen in some of the events described in this book.

Descendant
The seventh house cusp is always opposite the Ascendant and in the opposite degree and sign. This describes a spouse, significant other, business partner, doctor, client, enemy known to the person, perpetrator of a crime.

Detriment
A planet is in detriment when it occupies the sign opposite the sign that it rules. Venus rules Libra so is in her detriment in Aries. Planets in their detriment do not operate well with their basic natural energies because they are not in a comfortable environment within which to do so. Planets in detriment are disorganized. The easy, peace-loving energy of Venus is challenged when placed in Mars' fiery sign Aries, so she is in her detriment and can't function as she normally would; she becomes aggressive and demanding. In crime charts and event charts ruling planets in detriment show a loss of control and an inability to help themselves both in, and out, of difficult situations.

Dignity
Dignity is classified as either essential or accidental. It describes the condition of a planet and how well its energies function at a given position. Planets in their own signs of rulership or exaltation are said to be essentially dignified and have power in a chart and control over a situation. For example, Saturn rules Aquarius and is dignified in that sign as it works well through the energies of Aquarius.

Planets are also dignified by house placement or in relationship to other planets. They are said to be in their "joy" in certain houses and are thus accidentally dignified. Here is the chart of houses of the planetary joys:

Sun – Ninth House
Moon – Seventh House
Mercury – First House
Venus – Fifth House
Mars – Sixth House
Jupiter – Eleventh House
Saturn – Twelfth House

On the other hand, planets in their detriment or fall are not well dignified because their energies do not operate well within the confines of those signs. The peace-loving, pleasure-seeking Venus becomes aggressive and domineering in Mars' sign Aries, where she is in detriment, or in Scorpio, where she is in fall. In summary, planets are accidentally dignified by house placement and essentially dignified by sign placement. Please refer to Section 2 for the chart of sign rulerships, triplicities, terms, and dignities.

Dispositor
A dispositor is a planet which rules the sign that another planet is in. For example, if Jupiter is in Gemini, Mercury is the dispositor of Jupiter because Mercury rules Gemini.

Eclipse
An eclipse involves the parallel conjunction of the Earth, Sun and Moon. Specific degrees of an eclipse are very important in predictive and event astrology. Solar eclipses occur during the New Moon and Lunar eclipses occur during the Full Moon. See the article on the Haiti earthquake for discussion on eclipse points in relation to historic events.

Elements
The twelve signs of the zodiac are divided into four elements: Fire – Earth – Air – Water. There are three signs of each element, as follows:

Aries – Fire
Taurus – Earth
Gemini – Air
Cancer – Water
Leo – Fire
Virgo – Earth
Libra – Air
Scorpio – Water
Sagittarius – Fire
Capricorn – Earth
Aquarius – Air
Pisces – Water

By studying the sequence of signs you can see the progression of elements through the zodiac in the order shown above. Each element has specific qualities and forms what is called a "triplicity" of the signs. The fiery triplicity is Aries, Leo, Sagittarius, the earthy triplicity is Taurus, Virgo and Capricorn, and so on.

Elevation, Elevated
A planet is elevated when it is above the horizon and especially when close to the Midheaven or tenth house cusp.

Exaltation
A planet is well-placed when in the sign of its exaltation, which confers some degree of power to it. When representing a person in an event chart, a planet in its exaltation is powerful, sometimes undeservedly so. A king may be exalted because he is the ruler of a country, but that doesn't always mean he deserves the high esteem which he receives. It is power conferred on him by others.

Face
Divisions of a sign in sections of 10 degree each, or decanates, ruled by planets. See 2. Table of Planetary Dignities.

Fixed signs

The fixed signs are Taurus, Leo, Scorpio and Aquarius. General characteristics of these signs are steadfastness, durability, firmness and resistance to change.

Fixed stars

A fixed star is a celestial body which generates its own light, unlike a planet which is visible by way of reflected light. Fixed stars are so called because they progress extremely slowly through the zodiac, moving only about one degree of arc approximately every 72 years. Most of the fixed stars form constellations and have been known to man since the early days of stargazing thousands of years ago. Many fixed stars are associated with mythical stories and persons. They were considered to have a generally malefic influence but some fixed stars confer great destiny when well placed. When conjunct a planet or angle within one degree or less, a fixed star is significant: see discussions on the presence of fixed stars in the chapters on Charles Lindbergh, Jr., Marilyn Monroe, the the Air France Airbus and the Costa Concordia.

Grand cross or grand square

A configuration of four planets which form a shape of a cross, which can only occur in planets of the same quality. For example: Mercury in Pisces opposes Mars in Virgo, while Sun in Sagittarius opposes Saturn in Gemini. This forms a grand cross, or square, in mutable signs. This aspect is a very stressful aspect but a very dynamic one, as many energies are in conflict with one another. The orb of influence may range from three to seven degrees.

Grand trine

A formation of three planets of the same element which form a 120-degree angle. A grand trine in antiquity was thought to bring ease and harmony to the individual but was not necessarily always favorable, depending on the dignities of the planets involved. For example, Mars at 15 Libra trines Jupiter at 17 Gemini which also trines Saturn at 14 Aquarius. This is an example of a grand trine in the air element. The orb of influence may range from zero to seven degrees.

Horizon

The horizon is also called the Ascendant-Descendant axis. It divides the horoscope into upper and lower sections. The upper portion is Southern in direction and diurnal in time, the lower portion is Northern in direction and nocturnal in time.

Houses

There are twelve houses in every horoscope, each house representing a person, thing, group or life experience. Below is a rudimentary list for the beginner to study. For more extensive review of the rulerships of houses I invite the reader to study Rex E. Bills' *The Rulership Book,* listed in the **Bibliography**.

First house: the appearance, physical traits, state of health, personality. In a crime chart the victim is shown by the first house and in an event chart the subject of the inquiry or event is shown by the first house.

Second house: one's possessions, values, finances, money

Third house: communication, mental abilities, short trips, siblings, neighbors

Fourth house: one's home, family, end of a matter, the father, burial place

Fifth house: love affairs, creativity and creations, children, sex, pleasures, entertainment

Sixth house: servitude, illness, repairmen, domestic workers such as housekeepers, accidents, misfortune

Seventh house: Marriage or business partners, known enemies, one's doctor, relationships

Eighth house: Death, inheritance, taxes, anxieties, other people's resources or money

Ninth house: Religion, spirituality, universities, philosophy, law enforcement

Tenth house: Career, profession, public reputation, the mother

Eleventh house: friends, peers, goals and hopes, social groups

Twelfth house: Secrets, confinement, institutions of confinement such as hospitals, prisons, incarceration, secret enemies, sorrow

Lunar nodes

These are not planets, but points in a horoscope, much like the Arabic Parts or Lots. The Lunar Node, or Moon's Node indicates the degree of longitude at which the Moon passes over the ecliptic. The Moon's Node is either the North Node or the South Node, also called, Head of the Dragon (Dragon's Head) or Tail of the Dragon (Dragon's Tail), respectively. Planets which conjoin one of the nodes are very significant in an event chart. For example, in the event chart of the passing of Marilyn Monroe, Saturn was conjunct the South Node in the eighth house, and the reader is referred to that discussion of her death in Chapter I.

Malefic

A planet having an unfavorable influence. In medieval astrology Mars and Saturn were considered malefic planets which indicated difficulty, hardship and loss. However, any planet can have a malefic or negative influence if poorly placed in a horoscope. See the discussion in this Appendix on **Dignity**.

In a diurnal or day chart, Mars is more malefic in nature than Saturn. In a nocturnal or night chart Saturn is more malefic than Mars. The position and placement of these planets will also describe the quality or nature of these planets and how they operate in the horoscope. A well-placed Saturn is generally better than a poorly placed Venus. See also **Benefic.**

Midheaven

The Midheaven is the cusp of the tenth house, and is also called the M.C., for "medium coeli." It is the most elevated position in a horoscope; see also **Elevated, Elevation.** Its opposite fourth house cusp is called the I.C. or "imum coeli."

Mutable
Refers to the quality of the signs Gemini, Virgo, Sagittarius and Pisces, which are generally characterized as flexible, adaptable and changeable.

Mutual reception
When two planets occupy each other's signs of rulership, showing a relationship or willingness for one to assist the other in the areas that they rule. For example, Mercury in Libra and Saturn in Virgo are in mutual reception and so help each other in matters involving analytical work, writing or communication.

Mutual reception can also occur by exaltation; Mars in Pisces and Venus in Capricorn is an example of mutual reception by exaltation. When two planets are in reception by rulership and exaltation this is called mixed mutual reception: Saturn in Leo is in mixed mutual reception with Sun in Libra because Saturn occupies the sign ruled by Sun, while Sun occupies the sign in which Saturn is exalted.

Peregrine
A planet is peregrine when it is lacking in any essential dignity. A peregrine planet describes something hat is lost or lacking direction.

Planets
Planets are the celestial bodies in our solar system whose light is reflected, not self-generated like stars. That is why planets do not twinkle like the stars do. The planets of our solar system are Mercury, Venus, Earth, Mars, Jupiter, Saturn, Uranus, Neptune and Pluto. The Sun and Moon are not planets, but are collectively termed as such in this work for ease of reference. The Sun and Moon are more accurately referred to as the "luminaries" or "lights."

Traditional or classical astrology does not recognize the outer planets Uranus, Neptune and Pluto because those planets were not known to early astrologers. Modern astrology makes use of these outer planets and even assigns rulerships to them. In this work, as in my practice, I utilize the outer planets as descriptors, but do not consider them as rulers of the zodiac signs. In forensic and event astrology the outer planets generally have a malefic influence.

Progressions

A progression is based on the movement of a planet from the time of birth, or from a specific given time, to another time. Progressions are used largely in predictive astrology, and also to determine energies present at certain points during the lifetime. Refer to the Chapter I discussion on the death of Marilyn Monroe to learn more about the progressions in her natal chart to the day of her death.

For example, in the most common form of progressions used, secondary progressions, the Sun progresses one degree for each year of the life. If you were born with your Sun at 5 degrees Leo, at age 30 your Sun will have progressed to 5 degrees of Virgo.

Quality

The qualities of the planets are categorized as follows: Cardinal – Fixed – Mutable, and there are four signs belonging to each astrological quality.

Cardinal Signs = Aries, Cancer, Libra, Capricorn
Fixed Signs = Taurus, Leo, Scorpio, Aquarius
Mutable Signs = Gemini, Virgo, Sagittarius, Pisces

See also: **Cardinal, Fixed, Mutable**.

Rectification

Astrologers use a system of calculations based on important events in the life to determine the exact time of a person's birth; this process is called rectification of a chart. For example, using the date and time of a person's wedding, an astrologer can rectify a person's birth chart because certain planetary configurations are in evidence when a person marries, which can yield the information needed to cast the birth chart. This is an very skilled process and requires a great deal of expertise on the part of the astrologer.

Retrograde
This phenomenon occurs when a planet appears to be traveling backward in its motion from the point of view of the earth. The planet is not actually moving backward, but only appears to do so from here. Planets in retrograde are considered to be weaker than when they are perceived to be moving in direct motion, and matters they represent often experience delays and setbacks during the retrograde period. Mercury goes retrograde the most frequently, about three times each year, while the other planets also have retrograde periods at less frequent intervals. The Sun and Moon never enter into retrograde motion.

Rising
A planet on or near the eastern horizon of the chart, or Ascendant. For example, Venus is in Aries at 14 degrees while the Ascendant is 16 degrees Aries; Venus is rising.

Ruler
Each zodiac sign has a planetary ruler and each planet in traditional astrology rules two signs; the Sun and Moon, which are not planets in the true sense, each rule one sign:

Sun rules Leo
Moon rules Cancer
Mercury rules Gemini and Virgo
Venus rules Taurus and Libra
Mars rules Aries and Scorpio
Jupiter rules Sagittarius and Pisces
Saturn rules Capricorn and Aquarius

In traditional astrology the outer planets Uranus, Neptune and Pluto are not planetary rulers.

Separating aspect
A separating aspect has already completed its connection to another planet. For example, Venus at 27 Sagittarius separates from a square with Saturn at 25 Virgo.

Stellium
A grouping of three or more planets in the same sign or house. For example, Neptune, Mercury, Venus and Sun all in the sign Libra form a stellium in Libra.

Terms
Divisions of a sign which are ruled by planets. See 2. Table of Planetary Dignities.

T-square
When two planets which are in opposition form a square to a third planet, forming a t-shaped configuration in the chart. For example, Moon at 2 Leo opposes Mars at 5 Aquarius. Both are in square aspect to Saturn at 2 Scorpio, forming a cross or T-square.

Tight aspect
An aspect which is very nearly exact, within one degree on either side.

Transit
The passage of a planet in aspect to another planet or a specific point in a horoscope. For example, last year Saturn, which was transiting the sign of Libra, made a conjunction by transit with my natal Sun which is in Libra in my birth horoscope. Transits are often one of the bases upon which predictions are made, although other factors also need to be taken into account.

Trine
A 120-degree relationship between two planets belonging to the same element. For example, Moon at 12 degrees Capricorn and Venus at 13 degrees Taurus are in trine relationship to each other. The orb of influence may range from zero to seven degrees.
Triplicity – see Section 3.

Water signs
The water signs are Cancer, Scorpio and Pisces and this is called the watery triplicity.

Zodiac
The zodiac is the division of twelve sections or houses of a horoscope chart which relate to several different aspects and experiences of life. There are 360 degrees in a horoscope and traditionally the houses measured 30 degrees each, although there are many different systems that determine the boundaries or cusps of each house.

2. Table of Planetary Dignities

A Table of the Essential Dignities of the PLANETS according to Ptolemy

Sign	Houses of the Planets	Exaltation	Triplicity of Planets D / N	The Terms of the Planets					The Faces of the Planets			Detriment	Fall
♈	♂ D	☉ 19	☉ ♃	♃ 6	♀ 14	☿ 21	♂ 26	♄ 30	♂ 10	☉ 20	♀ 30	♀	♄
♉	♀ N	☽ 3	♀ ☽	♀ 8	☿ 15	♃ 22	♄ 26	♂ 30	☿ 10	☽ 20	♄ 30	♂	
♊	☿ D	☊ 3	♄ ☿	☿ 7	♃ 13	♀ 21	♄ 25	♂ 30	♃ 10	♂ 20	☉ 30	♃	
♋	☽ D/N	♃ 15	♂ ♂	♂ 6	♃ 13	☿ 20	♀ 27	♄ 30	♀ 10	☿ 20	☽ 30	♄	♂
♌	☉ D/N		☉ ♃	♄ 6	☿ 13	♀ 19	♃ 25	♂ 30	♄ 10	♃ 20	♂ 30	♄	
♍	☿ N	☿ 15	♀ ☽	☿ 7	♀ 13	♃ 18	♄ 24	♂ 30	☉ 10	♀ 20	☿ 30	♃	♀
♎	♀ D	♄ 21	♄ ☿	♄ 6	♀ 11	♃ 19	☿ 24	♂ 30	☽ 10	♄ 20	♃ 30	♂	☉
♏	♂ N		♂ ♂	♂ 6	♃ 14	♀ 21	☿ 27	♄ 30	♂ 10	☉ 20	♀ 30	♀	☽
♐	♃ D	☋ 3	☉ ♃	♃ 8	♀ 14	☿ 19	♄ 25	♂ 30	☿ 10	☽ 20	♄ 30	☿	
♑	♄ N	♂ 28	♀ ☽	♀ 6	☿ 12	♃ 19	♂ 25	♄ 30	♃ 10	♂ 20	☉ 30	☽	♃
♒	♄ D		♄ ☿	♄ 6	☿ 12	♀ 20	♃ 25	♂ 30	♀ 10	☿ 20	☽ 30	☉	
♓	♃ N	♀ 27	♂ ♂	♀ 8	♃ 14	☿ 20	♂ 26	♄ 30	♄ 10	♃ 20	♂ 30	☿	☿

3. The Triplicities

The diurnal planets are: Sun – Mercury – Jupiter – Saturn

The nocturnal planets are: Moon – Venus – Mars

The triplicities of the signs are by element. The first two planets switch places if the horoscope is nocturnal. See chart below:

ELEMENT DIURNAL NOCTURNAL

FIRE: Aries, Leo, Sagittarius	Sun – Jupiter – Saturn	Jupiter – Sun - Saturn
EARTH: Taurus, Virgo, Capricorn	Venus – Moon – Mars	Moon – Venus - Mars
AIR: Gemini, Libra, Aquarius	Saturn – Mercury - Jupiter	Mercury – Saturn - Jupiter
WATER: Cancer, Scorpio, Pisces	Venus – Mars – Moon	Mars – Venus - Moon

The reader is referred to Deborah Houlding's excellent article, "The Classical Uses of Triplicities," at www.skyscript.co.uk, and also the classical work Carmen Astrologicum by Dorotheus of Sidon.

4. Symbols of the Planets and Signs

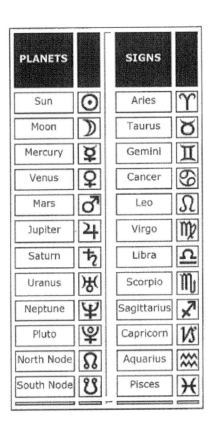

PLANETS		SIGNS	
Sun	☉	Aries	♈
Moon	☽	Taurus	♉
Mercury	☿	Gemini	♊
Venus	♀	Cancer	♋
Mars	♂	Leo	♌
Jupiter	♃	Virgo	♍
Saturn	♄	Libra	♎
Uranus	♅	Scorpio	♏
Neptune	♆	Sagittarius	♐
Pluto	♇	Capricorn	♑
North Node	☊	Aquarius	♒
South Node	☋	Pisces	♓

5. THE ARABIC PARTS (ALSO CALLED LOTS)

Some commonly used Parts are obtained by the following formulas. The Parts are often referred to in this book as having significance in describing events. The planetary ruler of the Part and its location in the horoscope also reveal important information about an event:

Part of Fortune: ASC + Moon – Sun
Part of Spirit: ASC + Sun – Moon
Part of Disaster: ASC + 8th cusp – Moon
Part of Peril: ASC + 8th cusp – Saturn
Part of Danger: ASC + Saturn – Moon
Part of Catastrophe: ASC + Uranus – Saturn
Part of Plane Crash: ASC + 9th cusp – Pluto
Part of Suicide: ASC + 8th cusp – Neptune
Part of Accident: ASC + Saturn – Mars
Part of Last Place: ASC + 4th cusp – Saturn
Part of Death: ASC + 8th cusp – Moon
Part of Destruction: ASC + Mars – Sun
Part of Damage: ASC + Neptune – Venus
Part of Poisoning: ASC + Saturn – North Node

6. Degrees of Danger

The following degrees are considered significant in interpreting horoscopes of events, and are called "critical degrees:"

4 and 17 degrees of mutable signs Gemini, Virgo, Sagittarius, Pisces

12 and 26 degrees of cardinal signs Aries, Cancer, Libra, Capricorn

8-9 and 21-22 degrees of fixed signs Taurus, Leo, Scorpio, Aquarius

29 degrees of all signs. The late degrees of all signs should also be noted because they fall in the terms of Mars or Saturn, traditionally considered malefic in effect. Zero degrees of the cardinal signs are called the "Aries point," which in modern astrology relates to a drive for publicity and public exposure.

22 degrees of all signs

15 degrees Leo is considered a very difficult placement by degree.

When a planet is within one degree of conjunction to a fixed star, this placement is critical. If the planet is Mars or Saturn, the effect is usually detrimental, and the meaning associated with the fixed star is enhanced. Fixed stars and their meanings have been discussed throughout this book and the reader is referred to the works in the Bibliography by Ebertin-Hoffman, Robson and Brady.

7. Bibliography and References

Al-Khayyat, Abu'Ali. The Judgement of Nativities, translated by James H. Holden, M.A., Tempe: American Federation of Astrologers, 2008.

Allen, Richard Hinckley. Star Names and Their Meanings, New York: G.E. Stechert, 1899.

Bills, Rex E. The Rulership Book, Richmond: Macoy Publishing & Masonic Supply Co., 1971.

Bonatti, Guido. The Book of Astronomy, translated by Dr. Benjamin Dykes, Golden Valley: Cazimi Press, 2007.

Carter, C.E.O. Some Principles of Horoscopic Delineation, London: L.N. Fowler & Co., Ltd.

Cornell. H.L., M.D. Encyclopaedia of Medical Astrology, St. Paul: Llewellyn Publications, 1972.

Ebertin-Hoffman, Reinhold. Fixed Stars and Their Interpretations, Tempe: American Federation of Astrologers, 1971.

Frawley, John. The Real Astrology, London: Apprentice Books, 2000.

Gilbert, Priscilla M. Potential Fulfilled: Accident Patterns, vol. I, Tempe: American Federation of Astrologers, 1976.

Heindel, Max. <u>Astro-Diagnosis or Guide to Healing</u>, England: L.N. Fowler & Co., 1929.

Houlding, Deborah. "The Classical Uses of Triplicities," www. skyscript.co.uk

Kennedy, Ludovic. <u>The Airman and the Carpenter</u>, New York: Penguin Books, 1986.

Lehman, J. Lee, Ph.D. <u>Essential Dignities</u>, Westchester: Whitford Press, 1989.

Lehman, J. Lee, Ph.D. <u>The Book of Rulerships</u>, Westchester: Whitford Press, 1992.

Leo, Alan. <u>Complete Dictionary of Astrology</u>, Montana: Kessinger Publishing, 2003.

Lilly, William. <u>Introduction to Astrology</u>. Original publication 1647, Delhi: A. Sagar Book House, 1993.

Margolis, Jay. <u>Marilyn Monroe: A Case for Murder</u>, Bloomington: iUniverse, Inc., 2011.

Norris, William. <u>A Talent to Deceive: Who Really Killed the Lindbergh Baby</u>, Columbia: Synergebooks, 2008.

Robson, Vivian E. <u>The Fixed Stars and Constellations in Astrology</u>, New York: Samuel Weiser Inc., 1969.

Rowland, Edna. <u>Destined for Murder</u>, St. Paul: Llewellyn Publications, 1995.

Rowland, Edna. <u>True Crime Astrology,</u> St. Paul: Llewellyn Publications, 1996.

Saunders, Richard. The Astrological Judgment and Practice of Physick, original publication 1677, Abingdon: Astrological Classics, 2003.

Simmonite, W.J. Arcana of Astrology, North Hollywood: Symbols & Signs, 1977.

Speriglio, Milo. Marilyn Monroe Murder Cover-Up, Van Nuys: Seville Publishing, 1982.

Teal, Celeste. Eclipses, Woodbury: Llewellyn Publications, 2009.

Watters, Barbara. The Astrologer Looks At Murder, Washington, D.C.: Valhalla Publications, 1969.

Wikipedia.org.

Wolfe, Donald E. The Last Days of Marilyn Monroe, New York: William Morrow and Company, Inc., 1998.

Zoller, Robert. The Arabic Parts in Astrology. Rochester: Inner Traditions International, 1989.

Made in the USA
Middletown, DE
28 June 2021

43254372R00076